WHEN THE OUTSIDE MEETS THE INSIDE

A True Account of Healing from Ritual Abuse

VICTORIA RIVERS

ISBN: 1492923710
ISBN 13: 9781492923718

I Remember You.
You came from my body.
Agonizing, bloody horror
That disgusted and excited my captors.
I thought I was paying again
For my sins.

I remember you.
You were their victims, too.
Children, adults, and animals
We shared the horror.
I remember the sounds and the smells of torture,
The absolute terror in your eyes,
The relief when death came.

I remember you.
You tortured me. You programmed me. You controlled my mind.
I remember your voices, your eyes, your hands, and your raucous laughter.
I remember the cues, the signs, and the instruments of torture.
I remember your greed for sadistic pleasure
And for money from the sale of my agony.

I remember you
You do not remember the horror.
You continue to live
Apart from yourselves.

I remember you
You offered kindness and friendship
As the memories came.

Your skill, caring, and love
Held me and gave me hope
When I would have otherwise given up.

I remember you
You, like me, remember the torture.
Your sharing of your struggle meant
That I am not alone.

I will always remember you.

TABLE OF CONTENTS

ONE

A LOVE STORY

Hope and dissociation are the reasons I am alive today. Until I was thirty years old, I was a victim of ritual torturers. The powerful gifts of hope and dissociation saved me when I was repeatedly pushed past my limits of survival. I am thankful that I was able to dissociate and that my hope for a better life never totally disappeared.

On June 19, 1984, a few days before the first meeting of the Outside and the Inside, I wrote in my journal about the beginning of my life: *I had the image of seeing me as a foetus. There is a lot going on all the time. Cells continue to divide, to grow, and differentiate. There is a certain order. It is like a work of art. But if the waters of the womb are too shallow, too polluted, and too turbulent, the journey of the foetus from conception to birth will be a constant fight to live. The birth process takes courage for the foetus. It does not intend to cause the mother pain. But there comes a point where the foetus needs, and must be born. She needs to leave the womb and discover the reality of the world. The baby may be born in the hope that there will not be the pollution, shallowness, or turbulence of the womb. But the baby is born into an even more polluted, shallow environment. The waters are stormier, the fight to survive even greater.*

Hope was with me from the beginning, like a molecular component in the building blocks of life. Hope is an immovable, constant knowing that life will get better. Hope is a connection to where I came from and where I will go. Hope is a spiritual connection to others who have suffered and gone beyond

1

their suffering. Hope is a gift, just as a bird's song, spring flowers, and a child's joy are gifts. Hope would not let my spirit die.

Throughout my life, my hope has been encouraged by the kindness of acquaintances, friends, and strangers who offered me a smile or a few kind words. There were many teachers, classmates, neighbours, store clerks, and others who gave me encouragement and gentle attention. Although most of me could not accept any kindness, there were a few parts that greedily absorbed kindness like it was food for a starving child. It was like a full seven-course meal to hear from a teacher that I had done well. Laughing spontaneously at a classmate's antics encouraged the hope. All kind words and actions helped the hope to remain alive.

Hope alone was not enough to survive. I also needed dissociation. My mind separated into thousands of parts that each held various fragments of the horrors of ritual abuse and the capacity to save what was essentially me. But I did not know it until the Inside, the world of the dissociated parts, met who I thought was me, namely the Outside.

On the same day that I wrote about the beginning of my life, I also wrote about the relationship between hope and dissociation: *One image for me in growing up was that of a mould-able cushion on the outside, with a child huddling in an empty, dark corner inside. The cushion adapted to meet every body's needs, to be sat on, to be hit, to always bounce back. However, the child inside felt every hit, slap, and trembled in fear. More and more the child yearned for another world, where there was light and warmth and love.*

But the child heard voices that said there is no other world; this is your condemnation, your hell for causing so much pain and for making the waters of the womb so stormy. You deserve this. The child cowered, despairing.

But there was another voice, a voice from inside her, the voice of the other world. When she heard that voice, that voice within her, the child felt connected to that other world, the world of warmth, light, peace, calm. She longed for that world. But the two voices conflicted, and, in time, the voices from outside silenced the voice from the inside.

The Outside is the me I presented to the world, the me trained by the perpetrators to function in the world and not know anything of the abuse, so that I could not tell. The Outside is the me that smiled without knowing that I constantly smiled, that went through the motions of living and made it look sincere, particularly to myself. The Outside had absolutely no awareness of any of the abuse I had experienced. The Outside rationalized that the deep anxiety, fear, and depression were due to weighing too much, having a poor attitude, and not working hard enough.

The voice from the Inside that was silenced refers to the world that was lost to me. The Inside is the system of thousands of dissociated parts that were created to survive the trauma. Each part held a memory of the ritual abuse. Each part had a survival job. Although parts from the Inside often directed the Outside to keep me as safe as possible, the Outside did not know of the Inside's existence until the initial meeting.

I have learned that the perpetrators of the abuse were sadistic pedophiles (SPs). The primary trainers were the two people who called themselves my parents. I eventually decided to call them SP1 (father) and SP2 (mother). They were part of a group of people who had orgies and rituals and made money from pornography and prostitution. They were motivated by the money I would make for them and the fact that my birth was registered and my death would need an explanation. It took considerable training, skill, and knowledge to torture me to the edge of death but not let me die.

The story of the Outside and the Inside follows. The story is about denial, shock, terror, depression, risk of suicide, paranoia, neglect, unwillingness to change, difficulty functioning, power struggles, self-loathing, loss of time, and severe conflicts. Periods of healing were followed by very dry spells of separation and estrangement, couched in terms of "getting on with life" and "not dwelling in the past." Eventually, the Inside's primal, raw need for attention could no longer be discounted or pushed away. Inside knew that healing was now or never. The relationship between the Outside and the Inside had to heal or the suicide programming would be successful. Due to the Inside's persistence, the Outside agreed to commit to working on the relationship, and a love story was born.

Two

An Ordinary Life

My birth certificate records my hospital birth in 1953. I was told that my father had returned from overseas after the war and had been given government funding to obtain his PhD. My mother had a university education and became a stay-at-home mother as was the postwar norm. One brother was born when I was two years old, the next when I was eleven years old. My family appeared to be the normal, middle-class, suburban family.

I used to believe that I had an ordinary life. I assumed that the family life at home was very much like everyone else's family. I thought that my parents were like other parents. I fully accepted the appearance of my life. I have since learned that appearances can be deceiving, and that being middle or upper class means that a lot can be hidden.

I assumed that others had an emotional life like mine. I was separate from my emotions. I assumed that one never talked about feelings or problems. Feelings changed suddenly, as if controlled by a switch over which I had no control. I thought others my age carefully monitored the emotions of their parents as I did. I was constantly and desperately working to look after and please others. I did not know about pleasing myself. I did not expect kindness. I thought "love" and "caring" were words that must be used when speaking about parents. I never expressed anger. I thought it was normal to believe I was at the mercy of people and events that life put in my path. I thought that others had the same self-view and world view.

I kept the cardinal rule of portraying the picture of an ordinary life. I never thought to question this rule. I knew that the loneliness, emptiness, fear, and despair that grew as I got older must be hidden. I did not have the words for this struggle. I knew it was my secret, and no one must know. I felt it was a punishment, a sentence for being such a bad person. Suicide, increasingly, became a recurring thought.

Thankfully there were some very important people in my life who befriended me and gave me caring, nurturing, hope, laughter, love. Perhaps they saw hints of problems and intuitively knew that I needed a friend or a parent. It was from other adults that I received caring and concern. I did not know what to make of others being so nice to me, and I usually did not trust them. But I did accept some kindness.

Ages Five to Eleven

Conscious memory of my life used to start at age five, which is when I attended a kindergarten a few blocks from home. I had trouble remembering the route to the kindergarten. I had difficulty understanding what the teacher wanted me to do. I was uncomfortable with the other children. I had difficulty manoeuvring in such a foreign and scary world.

My grade-one teacher was a very stern, overpowering woman. I tried desperately to please her. I knew from her terse expression that I was not meeting her demands. The harder I tried, the angrier she got. One day, this teacher took me by the shoulders, shook me, and yelled that I was stupid and that I would never "get anywhere." This teacher taught me that school was a scary, rigid, cold, controlling place where I had to work very hard to survive.

Fortunately, my grade-two teacher was kinder than my grade-one teacher. She realized I could not see very well and told my parents to have my eyes tested. My parents would have appeared uncaring if they ignored this request. Glasses surprised me. Streetlights were not just one big blur. There were actually words written on the blackboard. People on TV had expressions on their faces. Teasing and self-consciousness aside, glasses were one of the best things that happened to me growing up.

In grades one and two, I did not understand the rules or what was expected of me. I learned to guess with increasing accuracy. Teachers' instructions made no sense to me. I was motivated by constant fear to be as perfect as possible. By grade three I had learned that to survive at school was to be a good student—but not the best—to be quiet, to never get in trouble, and to appear happy. In grade three I got 100 percent in arithmetic problems twice, which I could hardly believe. The teacher, I think, hoped that this would encourage me. But my father was never satisfied with my marks, not even a perfect mark.

Relating to other children was a foreign experience for which I was ill equipped. During the preschool and primary school years, I had one friend who lived across the street. We still correspond at Christmas. As she grew up, she developed many other friendships. I wanted to be her only friend. I wanted to play only with her. I liked going to "call on" her, which I thought literally meant call her, so I would knock on the door of her family's home and yell her name. I did not like the games all the kids on the street played in the front yards. I was taller and heavier than other girls my age. I did not want to play the hide-and-seek games or climb trees or any of the other similar activities. I was a tentative, scared, quiet, shy child whose goals were always to avoid being in trouble and to minimize harm.

During school recess, I would stand with the other outcasts on the pavement near the school and wish that recess would be over before the teasers decided to take aim at me. I did not want to play soccer or baseball because I might make a mistake and be yelled at. I did not want to skip or play hopscotch with so many others around. I nervously waited for the break to be over, not knowing what to say to the other outcasts and wanting to be invisible.

At school I learned that one got in trouble for not learning lessons quickly, for lack of effort, for lack of excellence, for talking, and for breaking rules. Therefore, I pressured myself to learn quickly, to do my work very well, to try very hard, to be quiet, and to keep all the rules. I would not consider asking a question, as it might betray the fact that I did not know what I was supposed to know. I was so occupied with keeping the rules and doing everything perfectly that I did not think about what I was learning or enjoy school. I did not purposefully draw attention to myself. I had good marks, but not the best marks, as that would bring dangerous attention. School was not about learning and not about having fun learning or playing with other children at recess. School was about survival.

Adults would have likely seen me as an ordinary, pudgy, quiet, reserved child who worked hard. Teachers wrote that I was "conscientious." It was assumed that a child who smiled all the time must be happy. It was assumed that because I was a child of middle-class parents, with a scientist father and a homemaker mother, all was well in our home. Adults not involved in the ritual abuse who knew me or my family, including neighbours and teachers, would have believed the facade without question, as did I.

As a child, my feelings, attitude, perspective, and system of internal rules were all normal to me. I was like an actor who convinced everyone, including herself, that life was normal. But it was not normal. A child who is too quiet and good is not normal. A child who never tests any limits is not normal. Always fading into the background, to the point of disappearing, is not normal. Trusting no one is not normal. Never getting into trouble is not normal.

Would I recognize a child who was being ritually abused? Would I notice clues of inner terror? Would I detect that she had been programmed to appear normal? Would I know if this child's words and actions are guided by the principle of least harm? Could I see through her convincing act that hides the dissociated parts holding the secrets of torture? How could I know of her terror if she herself does not know about it? I wonder what would have happened if someone had seen through the picture I presented to the world.

From a casual glance, no one knows about the reality of a child's life. Assumptions are made on the basis of one's own life, cultural context, values, class, and gender. Only if one has regular contact with the child would one possibly see the signs of dissociation. Because I was quiet and "good," teachers did not pay me any special attention. So it was that as a primary school–age child, my life seemed as normal as anyone else's.

Ages Twelve to Eighteen

As an adolescent, I continued to present an "ordinary" picture of myself to the world. At age twelve, I was quite overweight. I was the biggest girl in my class. And it felt like I was the most teased girl in my class. I dreaded school. I had few friends. My marks were above average.

By age fourteen, I was anorexic. I was totally consumed by what I was not going to eat. I was no longer teased me about my size. Being anorexic gave me an all-consuming focus. I believed that the less I ate, the better I would feel, and that the depressed, hopeless feelings would be gone. There was temporary relief in the high of losing weight and seeing my body get smaller.

Being a teenager meant surviving a more complex world. People assume that a person who is fourteen is going through the appropriate developmental stages. Even though I was unaware of the many young parts inside, existing in a teenager's world was increasingly alienating, confusing, and complicated. The more complicated and the more foreign the world seemed, the harder the parts inside worked to survive.

During the first day of high school, I got lost trying to find my locker. I did not know the layout of the school, and the hallways seemed identical. I walked for miles, frantically searching, going past lockers that looked the same again and again. Asking for help did not occur to me. My frenzy increased. I did not know what to do. The pressure of having to find my locker was steadily increasing. I was sweating and terrified. It occurred to me that the only benefit was burning off calories. The search seemed endless. I eventually found my locker. The pressure and terror disappeared instantly. I had trouble finding my locker again, but less so, and I eventually learned my way around the school.

Social interaction was something to be avoided. In terms of school hierarchy, my acquaintances would have again been classified as the outcasts. I had a friend with whom I walked to school and occasionally spent time. Looking back, I realize that I could not identify or judge characteristics or qualities that I might like or dislike. I did not realize that I had any rights in relationships or that I could make choices about friends.

Boyfriends were terrifying, and I tried to avoid them. When a boy asked me to the prom in grade twelve, I thought I had to say yes. During the prom, I desperately wanted the night to be over. I did not want to be in that situation, the dinner, the dance, and the boat cruise afterward. I felt repulsed when he tried to put his arm around me.

I approached life as though my survival depended on constantly improving everything I did. There was a focus on the detail of all tasks, of striving for perfection in everything. I had to anticipate everything that might happen in order to be ready for anything and everything. I interpreted events, words, and comments as personal threats. Stories about drinking, drugs, and sex overheard in the school washroom scared me. I felt like a young child in an alien teenage world where I did not belong.

The Outside appeared to be a teenager who was coping with life. Inside, parts that had learned the superficialities of what a teenager is supposed to do directed the Outside. But I was not coping. I wrote poetry about wanting to die. I did not know why I felt so bad, so empty, and so lonely. I did not know what these emotions were. I had difficulty negotiating the world of a teenager and preferred to withdraw and isolate myself. There was a constant overload of rules, expectations, and increasing difficulty in minimizing harm. As the outside world got bigger, with more possibilities, more people, more places, and more to learn, the Inside was increasingly overwhelmed.

At age fifteen, a neighbour had started jogging early in the morning. I decided to start jogging. I like to think that I was a pioneer in the jogging/running movement. In 1968, jogging was unusual. People would call out unflattering comments and dogs would chase me, but eventually I could run a mile, and then farther and farther. I started to eat again. I have been running ever since. Running has helped me all my life. Although running was initially about burning calories, it became much more. Every day I ran away from home, perhaps for just half an hour, but I ran away. Running encouraged hope and helped to calm anxiety. Running was an important survival tool. Even at my most suicidal, I ran. It might have been all I did in a day of depression, but I ran. Running became a way to breathe, to see beauty, to have quiet, to think, to lessen the internal chaos. Running has been a survival tool and a healing tool.

Ages Eighteen to Twenty-Eight

At age eighteen, I had a "boyfriend" who was in his early twenties. I did not have a clue about such a relationship. I did not know how to say "no." I felt that I had no rights. I looked eighteen, but I had no skills or experience for such a relationship. I could not tolerate this man's sexual advances and ended the relationship.

When I was eighteen years old, my "family" lived overseas for six months, ostensibly due to my father's work. I met a young man who seemed to like me.

He sang. He laughed a lot. He seemed to have a degree of safety about him. I really liked him. After returning to Canada, I exchanged letters with him for four years. I thought that this meant we were boyfriend and girlfriend. It was the safest way to have a boyfriend. He came to Canada. I envisioned marrying him and moving back to his home. His visit ended. He returned to his home and married someone else. I was devastated. The Outside had trouble pretending I was not hurting. My mother reminded me not to let anything show. Inside parts were hurt because they let themselves get attached to him and because an escape route disappeared. The attachment was about young parts needing someone who cared and who could help me be safe. I had no idea about the complexities of an adult romantic relationship.

My parents told me that I would go to university. At age eight, I wanted to be a social worker when I grew up. My father said I would not be a social worker. In high school, I decided I wanted to be a writer. He said no. He decided that I would be a scientist. I countered with doctor and he agreed.

I took premed at the university, a four-year degree in chemistry and microbiology. I was deeply depressed. I gained weight due to binge eating. I did not have friends. I ran. I studied. I remember feeling very alone and being overcome with a strong sense of futility. Working for a biochemistry professor in his lab improved life somewhat, as I had a place with people who seemed harmless. I had a sense of never being able to do what I was really able to do. While I had good marks, I could not understand why my marks were not higher. I did not have the perfect marks necessary for acceptance to medical school. I now understand that Inside parts did not want me to go to medical school.

I got a part-time job working in a church. I had been involved in a local church where I felt accepted, at least more accepted than anywhere else. I had an idea of giving my life to help people, to serve God. I decided I would be an ordained minister. Since I had the church's support, my parents could not stop me. I went seven thousand kilometers away to study theology. I escaped.

I have often wondered why I have so little recall of the theological courses. I listened to lectures, did a lot of reading, worked hard on assignments, completed all the requirements, but retained less from this degree than from my first degree, and much less than my third degree. I gained and lost about forty pounds at least twice over the four years of study. I remember walking three miles home from school, constantly thinking of the lettuce and cottage cheese I would buy for supper, and planning how I would not eat the whole thing, and how having half an apple for breakfast was preferable to the whole apple. I also remember the shock of waking up at 5:30 a.m. running up a steep hill, wondering what I was doing, and then feeling sudden panic that I had done nothing on an assignment that was soon due.

During these four years of studying theology, I thought that I was training to be a great minister. I did not realize that I had no sense of myself. I made myself into what I thought was expected. I tried to look like I was devout, caring, and sensitive to others. I hid my total distrust of people, my depression, and my need to isolate myself. I had no sense of myself. I was a chameleon who reflected the picture I thought each person wanted to see.

At age twenty-eight, I did not know that events in the next the next few years would lead me to start to understand that my life was not ordinary.

THREE

INKLINGS

In July 1981, I became the minister of a rural church. I remember thinking that now I would feel better. Now that I was a minister, everything would be fine because I was dedicating my life to serving others. Being a well-trained doormat, the image of the servant was one I bought into readily. I did not expect criticism or conflict. I did not anticipate any problems. If I had enough faith in this God that I had studied for four years, then all the troubling feelings would be gone. As a minister, I would be able to please everyone. My fear of conflict would not matter, as being religious meant that there would be no conflict or anger. It did not occur to me that being the first woman minister might cause some problems, or that I knew nothing about the culture of a rural farming community. When parishioners arrived on my doorstep with their criticisms of the "inclusive language" I had been taught to use for services, the fear returned. It never left.

I had the expectation that I should know everything without ever learning about it. I was required to complete a yearly statistical report that was returned to the national church. I am sure that to this day the statistics of the whole church are incorrect because I had no idea how to do the survey. I had never led or attended a wedding, yet I presided at many. I had learned something about conducting funerals during a summer placement. It did not occur to me to ask other clergy for advice. I did not know about the tasks of keeping a home, but again did not ask for help. Rather, I pretended to myself and others that I had all the required knowledge and skills for everything I had to do. Pretence was the focus of life on the outside.

The task I most liked was writing the sermon each week. When I was able to keep the fear at bay, I liked the way the words came onto the page. I liked preaching about justice, tolerance, and hope. These ideals resonated within me at very deep levels. The role I liked least was the very public persona of a clergyperson and the expectation that I would be outgoing and entertaining.

In the fall of 1981, my father was diagnosed with stage four colon cancer. The fear in me increased. It was like my nerve endings were on fire. My mother expected me to look after him and her. I had a job three hours away that I was trying to do perfectly. My brothers did not help and did not seem to understand the seriousness of the disease. My mother said that she did not understand why my father did not smile even though he was so sick and in so much pain. I was uncomfortable with the kisses he gave me and how he talked to me when I visited him in the hospital. He had a lot of fear. I realized he was afraid of dying, and I, being a minister, tried to assuage that fear. On one occasion, I arrived at the door of his hospital room to witness an emaciated, weakened creature, whimpering like a wounded, trapped animal, struggling to free himself. I tried to help him, but he continued to struggle as if I was not there.

He died early in 1982. I remember seeing his corpse in the hospital bed. The IVs were still hooked up but not flowing. His perpetually tense jaw was relaxed. He was very small and yellow. All tension, anger, and fear had left. Lots of people came to the funeral. The minister described him as a world citizen. I had no feelings.

During the months following his death, I had lots of energy, lost weight, and worked hard. I tried to develop friendships with a few people. I drove four hours to play racquetball. I felt burdened by my mother's demands, but I tried not to let her get me down. I was given a kitten that climbed the drapes and almost drowned in the cistern. A parishioner, who was a farmer, patiently helped me plant a garden. She assumed that I would know to continue to care for the garden. However, I did not know that weeding and watering was required. Each morning, while I was at my desk, I watched a neighbour, an elderly retired farmer, walk by my garden on his way back from picking up his mail. The look on his face varied from vague amusement to disgust to hopelessness. I thought he was lost in his own thinking. Now I realize he was looking at my garden.

Slowly, from about June 1983, the walls started to crash. Nightmares came. I had health problems. I was depressed. I had difficulty remembering and concentrating. I ate in binges. I tried to be a good minister, but I had increasing difficulty motivating myself to work. I tried to look after my mother. I felt more and more fear. I isolated myself. I had difficulty relating to anyone. I frequently left my phone off the hook. I had difficulty getting off the couch to do any work. The only solace I had was playing a piano that a parishioner had stored in my home.

I started a journal. The entries from August 1983 to June 1984 record a deep depression, some effects of dissociation, and a prelude to the initial meeting of the Outside and Inside. Recurring themes in the journal during this time period are eating, my increasing weight, God, loneliness, despair, suicide, ideas for self-improvement, and desperately trying to understand and change what was wrong with me. Inklings from the Inside initially emerge fleetingly in the journal entries, and later they appear with increasing and alarming clarity, until I could no longer deny them.

My second journal entry, dated August 28, 1983, is about my fear of writing: *Sometimes I think about writing. Sometimes I feel afraid of the creative side of me. Perhaps the creative side is linked to the sexual side of me.* I was afraid of writing because of where it might lead me. Here was a clue that journaling might include writing about some of my fears including the subject of sexuality. It had not consciously occurred to me that never having or wanting a sexual relationship with anyone might be abnormal. In spite of the fear, I kept writing.

Many of the entries indicate a deep and intransigent depression. In September 1983 I wrote the following: *I have been very depressed lately. How, O God, do I offer to you the loneliness that makes me feel I want to die? I deal with it by eating compulsively, by sleeping, by thinking negatively about myself. Depression makes me feel like I am a very rotten person and need to punish myself. God help me.* Three months later, the sentiment was the same: *Sometimes I would rather not exist. I want to live in a suspended state where I wouldn't have to feel anything. Is this what it is going to be like for the rest of my life? Am I doomed to this emptiness, loneliness, exhaustion, restlessness, numbness, desolation? I have died many times, and I feel I am dying again.*

I was isolating myself and experiencing deep emotional pain. *I am aware of how vulnerable and rejected I feel. I really feel the need to protect myself. I end up cutting myself off from others. I feel like I don't know how to act around people. I feel so ugly and socially inept. I do wish I didn't exist. It's like I have this terrible pain inside me and I want to die. I feel like I have nothing left, like I have died again. I keep eating, but that isn't helping. Sometimes I think about suicide. It would be the ultimate escape. I wouldn't worry about my weight. I wouldn't worry about this terrific pain I feel. It's not that I hate anyone else. I hate myself.*

Journal entries about Mother reveal inklings of one of the most painful internal conflicts. On January 6, 1984, I wrote: *I seem to be better with another person in the house. Mom has been visiting. She has made meals. It is much more enjoyable.* One day later I wrote: *I have to watch spending too much time with my mother.* Three months later, this sense of not wanting to spend "too much" time with my mother had intensified to wanting no contact. I did not know why I wanted nothing to do with her. I just knew that even the thought of her terrified me.

My mother acted very hurt. She talked to neighbours, officials in the church, friends, my previous counsellor, and my current counsellor to discount what I was saying and to request that they persuade me to be nicer to her. It scared me to hear my counsellors say they had talked to her on the phone or in person. Visits from church officials whom she had visited also scared me.

I continued to struggle with a very strong urge to kill myself, which I did not understand. My journal entry from March 3, 1984, describes an attempt to convince myself to stay alive: *God, help me. I feel angry at myself, at church, at you. I feel so lonely I could die. When I die, I would like to feel like I have really lived. I don't feel like that now. Now, I feel very empty, even though I have eaten too much. My hunger is not for food, but for life. I don't seem to be getting that hunger satisfied. What am I doing wrong? What is wrong with me? I just want to be me, to offer what I have, and yet I don't seem to be able to do that. Sometimes, I do want to die, not painfully, but so I will not feel anything. I am called to be faithful. Faithful does not include suicide.*

Soon after that entry, I saw my doctor because I was afraid I would kill myself, and on March 7, I was admitted to the psychiatric ward. I was very nervous there. I could not sleep. I could not get out to run. The other patients scared me. A nurse told me that I needed help, but I did not need to be in hospital. I told the psychiatrist that I was suffering from effects of my job. A friend offered me a place to stay. I agreed to counselling with a minister. I had learned that I would not get the help I needed in a hospital.

Journal entries continued to point toward the truth. I wrote about my fear of the Inside on March 10, 1984: *I have so many tears, so much fear, anger, guilt. I am afraid of really finding out what is inside of me.* On March 11, I wrote the following: *I am still very uptight. I need stronger sense of myself, of what I think and what I want.*

I could not figure out what was wrong with me. On March 14, I wrote that I must be the problem: *The problem is not the situation, it is in me. I am not open. I don't let myself be vulnerable. I hate myself and today again I think about dying. What is my purpose? It isn't only living and working in a small town with all the pressures attached. It is me. Why can't I be happy, peaceful, content there and wherever I am?*

I did not return to my job. I stayed in the city with a friend, and continued to receive counselling. The distress continued, as documented on May 14: *On Saturday night, I felt so desperate. I overate like crazy and again wanted to die. Part of me still does. Why do I cry so much? Why do I ache?*

On May 28, 1984, I wrote about what the counsellor had told me: *You have the right to live. Me? I thought. Everyone else does, but not me. But I do! Tonight I imagined telling my mother that I am not accountable to her. I do not have to report to her of my whereabouts or activities. I have a right to my space and time. I will not let her deny me or define me. I am me, thank God, and I have a right to live.* This helped calm the suicidal thinking for a short time.

On June 12, 1984, a few weeks before the conscious memories started, I made the following journal entry. I did not realize that I was not only describing my feelings but actual occurrences. *I have had to protect myself from those who were supposed to love me, who I wanted to love me more than anything, but who never did. I feel as though my mother and father did not want me and did not love me. For me to live, now, I must let go of all that family stuff and strike out anew. I feel my rage at mom and dad who used and abused me to fill their emptiness, who stripped me of any power, feelings, space, time, who took away my dignity, who buried me. I feel the rage and I do not know what to do with it. Let me out of the cage, the cage I have been in much too long. I want to live. I will no longer let others abuse me and deny me what is rightfully mine, namely me.*

On June 15, I wrote about the chaos inside and my mother's denial: *There is a lot happening inside of me, like things are shaking loose, things that I have needed to say for a long time, but were silenced. How was I to know anything different? What was real to me was abuse, put-downs, being silenced, and a hell of a lot of suffering. I thought that this suffering was my lot in life. Now, I am beginning to understand. My father was very angry and abusive. I am convinced he was alcoholic. What makes it so rotten is all the pretensions, including my mother's constant denial that everything was OK, nothing was wrong, everything was normal.*

The inklings were becoming stronger. I was somewhat more conscious that my parents were part of my problem. Something in me was changing.

FOUR

THE FIRST MEETING

A t the suggestion of my counsellor, I had several sessions of therapeutic massage. During the first few treatments, I had images of being bruised and bloody. With each treatment, the images and accompanying fear were more vivid and real. Initially I rationalized that the wounds were emotional. As the treatments progressed, the nightmares were more vivid, and I had an increasing sense of being more than emotionally wounded.

On June 26, 1984, I wrote the following: *I continue to wonder if I have ever been physically beaten or punched, if I have ever been the victim of violence. I don't remember any incident, but it plagues me, punched right in the guts. Perhaps I should ask for a massage to my "gut" area, maybe there is something to that. I don't want to try to remember something that isn't there. On the other hand, if it is there, I need to remember it. I think what the dream said is that there is something absolutely horrifying that I am not letting myself look at, but that, to heal, I need to look at. And, I don't know what that is.*

I asked for a massage of my abdomen at the next massage appointment. I was in another place. What was happening to me? There was nothing to see, only the overpowering sense of a penis being forced into my vagina. I could not move. There was a sense that this was all there was, the pain and terror. And then I found myself on the massage table. I was paralyzed with horror as I started to realize that this powerful body memory revealed that I had been raped.

19

On July 4, 1984, I wrote: *The massage last Friday really changed things. It feels awful to even write this, but I had a sense that I had been pinned, unable to kick or move my arms, unable to scream and was raped. Then, I thought I was going to die. Now, I feel like a little girl, so horrified and afraid and alone.*

The Outside had met the Inside. The me that I had always thought I was had met the me that was totally separate from my conscious mind. The Outside did not know of any abuse or violence or horror. The Outside appeared to function very well. This appearance hid the fact that the Outside did not know what I needed, wanted, thought, liked, or felt. The Outside focused on anticipating the needs, thoughts, and feelings of others. The Outside had no rights. In order to keep up the appearance of being a well-adjusted person, the Outside had to remain totally unaware of anything from the Inside.

The Inside was a world of dissociated parts that held memories of horrors and programming and parts created to help with survival. My abusers expected that this dissociated Inside world would stay separate, so that I would never consciously know what they had done to me to control my mind.

Even though the meeting had happened over a couple of years, it was immensely overwhelming. I would never be the same again. Shock and denial came in waves. The terror was constant. The shame was intense. My life was at stake. The first memory of being raped opened the floodgates, and other memories overwhelmed me. On the Outside, I did not know what to do. Lying down triggered memories, and I could not sleep for a month. When I went for a run, I felt the penis between my legs. I had trouble eating. I could not explain what was happening to me. I could not control the flashbacks. Nothing made sense. I lived in constant fear.

"Who did this to me?" I asked myself. The momentarily undeniable reality that my father raped me was quickly followed by waves of denial and disbelief. It could not be true. Loud words in my head said, "He was a scientist. He was respected around the world in his field. This cannot be. It must have been a neighbour." The denials were accompanied by pictures of parents and the home I remembered. At the same time, the body memory of his penis on the inside of my leg, a child's leg, and inside me, a child's body, was constant.

The battles in my head were intense and continued. One moment I believed that the disgusting memories and pain would go away and my familiar world would return. How could I have been raped by my father and not know? This made no sense. The next moment it was all true. I wanted all the memories to go away, yet I also felt some relief and some hope.

This crisis took over my life. On the Outside, I had difficulty talking to friends about everyday things. I went running, but I felt very unsafe. I could not predict when my body would shake uncontrollably. When I tried to lie down to sleep, the flashbacks and horrible feelings were more intense. I did not sleep for over a month. I forgot to eat. I had a small snack late at night and did not overeat. I felt like I was not really present. At night I was acutely aware of every sound for the entire night.

Eventually, the Outside accepted that my father had raped me. I told friends that I was a survivor of incest. I was relieved that this had been my problem all along. It explained the depression and anxiety. The Outside me felt that the worse was over. What could possibly be worse? Surely, things would go back to normal now.

FIVE

SHAKING OF THE FOUNDATIONS

The worst was not over.

What does one do when one's whole world is turned literally inside out, when absolutely everything about one's life is called into question? The Outside me acknowledged that this new information was important and believed that the effects on my life would be minimal. I tried very hard to ignore the waves of memories, which felt strangely separate from me and could sometimes be kept at a distance and temporarily forgotten. After ignoring the horror for a short time and desperately hoping that there was no more, the memories would come in an undeniable way. I had to pay attention.

I kept away from the person I then called my mother. I did not know why. Any form of connection with her, even the mention of her from others, resulted in terror. It was imperative that I have nothing to do with her, and I had no choice but to comply. I tried to deny that this was a significant change. I reassured myself that many women have issues with their mothers.

After about six months, I could no longer convince myself that life was back to normal. The Outside was drawn into the chaos Inside. I was not functioning well. I could not cope at work. I left my job. My savings were enough to support myself for a few months. After a few months, I received a disability pension. I found a reasonably priced apartment that felt as safe as anywhere.

I lived in my apartment for about four years. I did not know how to make a nice home for myself. I had an uncomfortable secondhand bed. My dresser was a cardboard box. In the second bedroom I had my desk, which was difficult to reach due to a sea of cardboard boxes that covered the entire floor. In one corner of the large living room I had an old, small, black-and-white TV at the end of my new couch.

TV helped to put the overwhelming chaos temporarily on hold. Watching the TV was a very important way of numbing myself so that I would not feel anything or think about anything except the vacuous TV program. Hours would pass in front of the TV as I tried to be rid of the world around me and the world inside me. Eating too much while watching TV provided temporary, partial relief.

Hearing my phone ring caused intense panic. I unplugged it. Leaving the phone plugged in meant that the most dangerous person in the world could reach me at any time. An answering machine provided assurance to friends who worried about me, but it did not help me. I needed to know that no one could reach me by phone.

I had several friends who had decided they would support me. Sometimes I felt like I was in a haze of unfamiliarity. I did not seem familiar to myself. I knew that I knew my friends, but there was an unreality to them. Sometimes I felt that I was stuck in endless, ever-deepening muck. Occasionally, there was a brief reprieve of feeling better and that life was worth living.

My day usually started with a run. For breakfast, I self-righteously restricted myself to a piece of toast or two pieces of low-calorie toast and coffee. I vowed each day to lose weight. And then I wrote. Words that described horrifying, tortuous scenes appeared on the pages my journal. I wrote thoughts, memories, and feelings that described an evil, twisted world unknown to me and yet known by me, a world that had to be a lie and at the same time was the absolute truth. I put in the rest of the day swimming, walking, having lunch with one of my few friends, and sleeping. At 5:00 p.m. I allowed myself to watch TV. I "numbed out" for the rest of the day, which usually included binge eating in the evening. I went to therapy once a week. On Sundays, I usually went to church. This was my life for about four years.

The journals of those four years are written in a variety of handwriting styles. They contain my words about the recurring themes of memories of torture, wanting to die, nightmares, self-hatred, depression, exhaustion, wondering what was true, short periods of relief, isolation, difficulty with relationships, and hoping against hope that I would soon be better and able to return to work and that the horror would be no more.

My journals record short periods where I was trying to convince myself that the worst was over, that there were no more memories, that I was whole and healed and able to get on with life as others seemed to do. In August 1984, I wrote: *I feel for thirty-one years, I have only been a very small part of myself—traces only of what is really inside me. I have come back to myself after needing to leave so long ago.* By mid-September, I wrote about memories: *I am on the cold cement basement floor, no clothes, my head pressed on the floor. He is pushing my head down, and fiddling with my rectum. Sometimes someone else is there. I feel torn and taunted. I feel—excuse the language* [always the polite person, even in my journals]—*all fucked up and damn angry.*

I did not want to know these things. Occasionally, the memories and terror would disappear, and I would have a brief reprieve. I hoped that the memories had ended for good and life would be manageable again. Then the floodgates of memories would open again, and I would want to die. I would be overwhelmed by memories of terrifying and revolting violence. I needed to be numb. I did not know what to do with these memories.

On September 28, 1984, I wrote: *I think that I have not yet begun to touch the depth and extent of the torture that I have endured. I know there is something more, much more. I was hung me upside down with him pressing my chest so much I thought he would crush me. Someone was threatening to drive nails into me, to put me in a drawer. He strangled me with his hands until I passed out. He burned me with matches and cigarettes.*

It was not until twenty years later that I would understand what I wrote about. October 13, 1984: *Why is it at some level I always feel I am being kicked, raped, and torn apart? Today strange things were going on with me. It was like my body was not my own. I was amazed that my legs moved. It was like I was watching them. Yet my knees were sore. I felt like I didn't have anything below them. And I felt I didn't have arms either. Sometimes it's like I have voices haunting me, voices laughing at me, voices telling me how bad I am, voices telling me that I would die that night, voices saying, "You're not much good at this. We are going to have to give you lots of practice." Sometimes it seems like there are three people there, three adults, raping, abusing me, and doing things to each other. It's like one raped me orally, one raped me, both at the same time. Could that be true? Unreal, I would say, yet my body seems to say it is true.*

I wrote about pieces of the memories I did not fully retrieve until about twenty years later. The entry of November 26, 1984, concerns a major technique that the programmers used: *I wonder if they really used electric shocks. Is that true? They wouldn't do that would they? I must be making it up. But it doesn't seem to want to go away.*

On June 26, 1985, I wrote about memories that would later present themselves as intense chest pain: *I very much want to die. I feel like I am being raped. Someone is stepping on my face. He cuts off my air supply. There is tremendous pressure on my chest and stomach.*

Journal entries from late fall 1984 include the topic of multiplicity: *I am very tired of all the different people I seem to be. … I am very disjointed, like I am many different people, depending who I am with. I feel I have many missing pieces. I am so suspicious of everyone, yet I can bluff my way through. I feel close to death, yet I look very healthy. I hate myself, yet come across as caring to others. I feel very weak and vulnerable, but give the impression of strength.*

A year later the theme of dissociation continued: *I feel disconnected, like I am in separate parts. … I have been thinking how much I have lived from the perspective of a terrified child. It is time to grow up!*

In many of my journal entries, I questioned how all this information remained hidden for so long could. I expressed my struggle between my sense that my memories were not real and my knowing that they *were* real. I wrote about my emotions being disconnected from my experiences. I wrote about hating feeling depressed and lethargic. I wrote about how much I hated myself.

I tried to make some sense of the brutality I was remembering. On November 30, 1984, I wrote: *Hell is the betrayal of human love.* A year later I wrote about evil: *Evil must be confronted, if human beings, including me, are to be free. That is tricky, though, because evil is so easily disguised. Evil has to do with torture and death. It has to do with human beings causing the torture and death of other human beings, who are powerless to fight. Evil robs people of what is rightfully theirs. Evil is never clear-cut and direct. It is insidious and pretends to be weakness.*

Therapy during this four-year period was helpful in several ways. During my first meeting with my therapist, she completed an assessment that included questions about my emotional state. It was very helpful to be asked about my anxiety and depression. The questions indicated that here was someone who understood and that I was not the only one who experienced these feelings. This was very encouraging.

My therapist believed me about the abuse. I had never told anyone about the violence, including myself. Since I was trained to deny the truth, it was vitally important that my therapist believe me. Her belief in what I said was basic to my relationship with her.

The relationship with my therapist helped me to not commit suicide. The pull to kill myself was present almost constantly throughout this four-year period. The concern and caring of my friends and my therapist helped to keep me from activating many plans of suicide. They helped stronger parts hang onto the hope, thus thwarting what I later learned was suicide programming.

As therapy progressed, my therapist pushed me to remember every detail of the assaults. Both the Outside and Inside resisted this. She asked again and again, wanting graphic details. Because of the fear of what might happen if I did not tell, I told. I felt like I was going through the incident again. I was back in time, being assaulted again. I could not tolerate the process. Well before the end of the four years of therapy, the processing of memories stopped. While fragments of memories continued to take me back, I could not, in detail, go through the remembering in therapy. I felt that I was giving myself surgery. It was just too hard.

I told my therapist that I had many parts, including many kid parts. In the mid-eighties, the issue of childhood sexual abuse was being revisited. A current understanding of the psychological phenomenon of dissociation and multiple personality as it related to childhood sexual abuse was in its infancy. My therapist did not understand what I was saying. Inside parts heard her saying she did not believe they existed. The crucial belief that she originally displayed was shattered. The Inside shut down communication with her.

Although therapy was not going very well, there was someone very positive in my life. I had found my partner whom I loved and trusted. Most of my

Inside parts felt safe with her. The caring, kindness, and stability I received from my partner were and are important factors in my healing.

Near the end of therapy, I developed a mononucleosis type of illness and was in bed for about six weeks. I lost twenty pounds, had fevers, wept each evening, and had a bad cough. In retrospect, I wonder if this was related to memories. I recovered, but for years, during extreme stress, I felt the same kind of exhausted weakness as I did during that illness.

At the end of this four-year period, I was somewhat better. I had happier moments. I functioned better in the world. I was able to work part time. I was able to be in a committed relationship. We moved to my partner's home province, away from the city in which I had grown up, a city I was glad to leave. I knew there was much of the horror I had not touched, and I hoped that I had done enough so that I would not have to remember any more.

SIX

A DISQUIETED TRUCE

I wanted a "normal" life. I had spent four years immersed in horrors. I knew that there was more. I wanted to believe that I was more or less all fixed. Following the completion of four years of therapy after the initial meeting of the Outside and the Inside, I had a fourteen-year span where I had a home, a partner, and co-parented my partner's granddaughter. I was working, and I returned to university to complete my second master's degree. I vehemently denied anything to do with parts of me, even when my partner pointed them out. This was as "normal" as it got for me.

The Outside tried to be the same as I was before any conscious meeting with the Inside. However, I could not always hide from the Inside terror. For example, while preparing to cross-country ski, a ski fell over. I found myself frantically rushing in different directions, not knowing where to hide. I heard my loud, heartbroken sobs. On another occasion, I was unable to find a sock. Inside parts switched so fast that my head was swirling. I could not believe the anguished screams that I heard were mine. There were other similar incidents throughout this "normal time." As I wrote on March 4, 1989, *Part of me says I am fine, but something underneath the surface is really hurting.*

Contact with biological family members, particularly my mother, triggered turmoil that could not be dismissed. Several weeks prior to a visit with my mother, and for some time after, I would be in emotional crisis. My fear level was very high. I had difficulty coping with everyday tasks. I constantly felt that too much was being asked of me, even if it was a very small request. I could not enjoy anything. I wanted to get away and I did not know what I was getting away from. On October 9, 1990, I wrote about the inner crisis provoked by contact my mother: *I have been immersed in "the shit" again. The cries, howls, noises that come out of me are really something. The children in me do have a lot to say, a lot of emotion, pain. The trouble is there is so much. I don't know what do to with it all.* Eventually the crisis would pass, and things would settle down again until the next contact with any biological family members.

A very difficult situation at work triggered extreme fear. I felt that three men, my supervisor, the executive director, and the chair of the board were ganging up on me because of political differences in a troubled organization. I went into survival mode. I was back in time to the ritual abuse, which I would not consciously know about for several years. Yet some of the truth was evident in my journal entries. In April and May of 1990 I wrote the following: *I think my fear has to do with the three of them, not knowing what they are doing, afraid of what they can do to me and have, in fact already done. … I have to reprogram myself. I know I was brainwashed. I have to tell the teenager part of me that I am safe. … The child parts need to be heard. I hear the most horrifying scream—like in a torture camp. There was more than just my daddy. Why do I have the feeling of eating warm gushy, blood stuff with lumps? There were group of men. They said, "We have decided that you have been so bad that you deserve to be punished. You will never get away from us."*

During my problems at work, my journal entries between August 1990 and January 1991 were also about multiplicity: *I resent the fact that I was so badly abused and therefore have so many parts. It's the terror that I hate. … Sometimes, I am so changeable. … My paranoid self is very close. It feels like she wants to take over. … I have many different parts of all different ages, as in multiple personality disorder. I don't think it is a disorder. It is just who I am.*

Various other incidents triggered an extreme fear reaction. When a passerby stopped to complain about our dog chasing her car, I was terrified that something bad was going to happen. I went to a lawyer to find out about our rights. When I had to deal with angry clients at work, I felt that my life was in danger. I remember driving into a gas station where there were many cars and trying to figure out who was next. When I thought it was my turn, I pulled up to a pump. After an angry man yelled at me for cutting in front of him, I could not get out of there fast enough. Following these and other incidents, I had days of turmoil and intense fear. I developed severe migraine headaches, painful arthritis, and a period of high blood pressure.

By about 2000, the anxiety, fear, and turmoil were increasing. My partner's fifteen-year-old granddaughter was acting out, resulting in increasing tension at home. The nice, fun times we had were gone. I did not feel safe at home. I felt desperate, chaotic, conflicted, and confused. I was extremely tense and on high alert. I wanted to leave, but I could not bear to leave. I desperately wanted my partner, but I did not know her. I was forgetful. I had difficulty eating and sleeping. I had increasing difficulty functioning. I had the feeling that I did not know what I was doing and I did not know what was happening to me.

My journals record deep, profound distress that did not make sense to me. I felt that the cause of my distress must be due to co-parenting a disturbed teenager with a partner who had disabling health problems. I felt unsafe at home. My journal entries from early in 2000 indicate that I did not tolerate this lack of safety well. On January 27, 2000, I wrote: *I am so tired and worn out. I am beyond exhaustion. When I do a check of my body, I don't even feel my body. With Jean, I also feel very uncertain, crazy, not sure who I am or who she is. I am not sure if the ground will be there to meet me when I fall, or if I'll keep falling, endlessly drifting. ... I feel powerless in my own home and home isn't home anymore.*

This was a very painful time for my partner, who felt that she had two troubled children, her granddaughter and me. She did not know what was happening to me, just as I did not know what was happening to me. I felt like I was desperately searching for her but could not find her. Yet she was right there, more than willing to help and needing support and love herself. I did not understand any of that. I was beyond that, in a life-and-death struggle that I did not consciously know.

Jean felt like I was very distant and wondered if I wanted to leave the re-lationship. My journals record my internal dialogue about staying or leaving. I wrote about feeling very anxious about our discussions. I anticipated what Jean wanted me to say and said it, because I did not know how I felt. I sometimes felt that the only reason Jean wanted to live with me was because I did so much work at home and I had a full-time job.

Occasionally, as in the journal entry of February 10, 2000, the love I felt for her was profoundly, but temporarily, present: *I feel that it's all I can do to prevent myself from coming apart totally. I don't know who to trust, what is real, what to do, where to go. Nothing I do or think of seems to address my pain and suffering. The last thing in the world I want to do is hurt anyone, most of all Jean. Please Goddess, help her heal from my thoughtlessness and heartlessness. I'm not totally sure what I have done wrong to her, but it must be pretty bad. She feels I am pushing her away, which I likely am, but I don't know her. I feel like I have never been here before. I don't know where I am. Things don't seem real. I am breaking apart inside.*

It was like the Outside had little or no control. The cyclone on the Inside swept up the Outside, picking up speed and wreaking havoc. The Inside saw threats everywhere, expected torture, and was working to survive the escalating onslaught. In February and March of 2000, I wrote about the chaos: *Goddesses, I increasingly desperately need your help. I feel alone, unlovable, inadequate, and ugly. I am spinning my wheels and I can't seem to stop. I am having trouble breathing. I want out of the jail inside me. I must get out or I'll die in here. So, Goddesses, walk with me out of the jail, a jail I have very likely created for myself. Jean says don't blame her for how I feel, that she didn't do anything. … I am many voices inside, many thoughts, many directions, and many conflicts. I am pulled in many directions from within and without. … My real problem is not home or work or where I want to live. The problem is that I am so separated out. I am going in so many directions. I am having increased difficulty holding everyone together. I can't function like this much longer. Some are getting stronger.*

I realized that I needed help. I had a vague sense that my problem was not due to tension at home or pressure at work. I tentatively started to understand that the problem was in me. Through benefits at work, I met with a counsellor. During the two sessions, parts switched quickly. I could not answer the counsellor's questions because the part who heard the question was not present to give the answer. The counsellor, who did not understand what was happening, repeated the questions, as if I were forgetful or unfocused. I realized that my problem had to do with all my parts and that I needed help from a therapist who knew about multiple personality disorder. I remember feeling that I did not even have to like the therapist as long as she knew how to help me.

I nervously phoned a sexual assault centre in hopes it would have the name of a therapist who worked with DID (dissociative identity disorder). I was told that there was a therapist at the centre who worked with clients who were multiple. I did not know how fortunate I was to find a person with this expertise.

SEVEN

BEGINNING THERAPY, AGAIN

Therapy sessions with Pat were two hours long, every two weeks. During sessions, I listened to myself say the most foreign, absurd, strange-sounding statements. Powerful feelings from unknown depths would overwhelm me. The intensity scared me. I learned to feel the emotion at a much reduced intensity so that I could release it. I needed therapy to keep me on track, to guide me, to teach me, to encourage me. I always felt in need of the next therapy session.

On March 23, 2001, during my first session with Pat, she asked, "Do you know about your system?" I was puzzled. The Outside me had no idea about an Inside system. I did not know how many parts were Inside, what their various jobs were, how they related to each other, or how they were created. I did not know that many of the parts were intentionally created by my parents and other trainers who programmed parts for certain tasks. I did not understand that some parts were created in life-and-death moments to help me survive. I came to understand that "my system" referred to the world of parts Inside and how it was organized.

While I did not know anything about my "system," I did know that the Inside was in chaos. I was becoming aware that I would lose time. I experienced switching from one part to another at such a rapid rate that it was like a turnstile spinning at breakneck speed. However, I did not want to acknowledge any parts. I had spent the last fourteen years studiously avoiding as many parts as possible. I was afraid to know anything about these parts. I wished they would disappear and I would feel better. Yet I could not continue as I was. My therapist persuaded me that getting to know about these parts would help with the distress and chaos that overwhelmed me.

The concept of actually listening to the multitudes Inside was disarming. My previous experience at reliving the memories in therapy had been unbearably difficult, and I could not do that again. Pat was not talking about memories, though. She was talking about getting to know the parts. This was not as scary. I did not want any memories, but perhaps I could handle meeting parts. Because I was desperate for some relief and did not know what else to do, I decided to listen to the parts. It was fortunate that at this time I had no idea that the parts would number in the thousands.

As I recorded on March 24, 2001, I started to listen to the Inside: *There is still chaos, but more hope. I need to listen, but one at a time. I can't hear a cacophony. Maybe what I have is clusters, or families. For a very long time, I haven't listened. Now the "I" gets lost. Did I have a baby? What happened? Maybe now I'll know.*

Over the next months, I met some of my system. I needed a family, and found I had many Inside families. There were many groups of parts I called families as well as individual parts. Families were groups of very similar parts, gathered together for a specific function. The name of each family indicated its function. I recorded their names in a special notebook.

The "Intuitive Ones" had wisdom and knowledge of the whole system and its parts. The "Denial Family" worked hard to protect me from knowing anything. Related to it was the "Peers Happy Family" and the "I Love My Parents and I Have a Good Family Family." Some of the emotional pain was taken by the "Fear Family" and the "Anger Family," which included the eight-year-old "Grr Boy," the "Screaming Club," the "Bloodcurdling Noise Club," the "Crying Club," and the "Brokenhearted Family." The "Watchers" and the "Guards" were always on duty. Some of the other groups included the "Jail People," the "Dead Ones," the "Faker Family," the "Invisible People," the "Silent Ones," the "Gatekeeper," the "4 Happy Family" (happy on one side and shit, urine, vomit, semen on the other), the "Hanging Ones," the "Copy Family," the "Pretender Family," the "Stopping-Up Family" (constipation), and the "Heroines."

Getting to know my system and starting some preliminary communication was surprising, shocking, and strangely familiar. Thankfully, it was not too difficult. It was astonishing to learn there were so many parts. I could see the parts and the families. They were real to me. During therapy sessions, the communication improved. Pat was teaching me to communicate by listening to the parts and telling them what they needed to hear. Throughout my seven years of therapy, she repeated, "You are a good person. You got away. You escaped."

As the communication between the Outside and the Inside improved, parts were telling me pieces of what had happened to them. I had dreaded this for years. On May 2, 2001, I wrote about what I had been dreading: *Yesterday, I realized that I/we will need to do some remembering of the abuse, hopefully in a more manageable way than fifteen years ago, so that those who have the memories, who have been keeping them all these years, can be free.*

Pat explained that I could learn how not be so overwhelmed by the memories. She suggested that I could learn to feel the emotions at a much reduced level. In time, the Inside cooperated and would calm the emotion so I could tolerate it. When a part wanted to tell, Pat would gently encourage me to listen. To my great relief, she did not push me to describe every detail. She let the bits and pieces come. And I slowly learned that I could handle remembering.

For the second time in my life, but in a more informed way, I committed myself to healing. The Inside and Outside would learn together about healing. The decision to commit regular time to listen to my many parts was vital. The agreement was that I would pay attention to the Inside when writing and running early in the morning, and they would not appear when I was at work. Writing and running have been central to my healing.

I continued with writing in my journal most mornings. I learned to let words come onto the paper. Initially, I judged and censored the words, because they seemed impossible and nonsensical. I learned to write it anyway. Listening meant accepting what came and trusting that the truth would appear. Much of what I had written during my first years of therapy about twenty years earlier appeared again.

In addition to writing most mornings, I ran for about half an hour. During my run I listened to the Inside and talked to the parts silently or aloud.

Running was important to all of me, and it seemed to help me keep on a more even keel. Inside parts came to trust that they would have time each morning and had less of a need to push through when I was at work. The running was a reminder that I was free, that I could move and feel my physical strength.

My body had so many pains that there were many times when I wondered if I was seriously ill, but the symptom would pass. I eventually learned that much of the body pain was memory and that my body had been trying to let me know for a very long time. My therapist helped with further skills in listening. She listened to me, offered education, and normalized what seemed very frightening and bizarre to me.

Occasionally, I could not handle the horror and intensity I was feeling, and I could not wait for the next session. I felt the only way to help calm the crisis was to phone Pat. I knew I could phone her at her office, including after hours when I could ask the emergency worker to ask her to call me. Hearing her calm, reassuring voice calmed the Inside terror. After a several years of therapy, I learned to do this for myself.

Beginning therapy again had a big impact on my relationship with my partner. I did not realize that I was seldom the person that Jean knew. Jean needed the support that I was seldom able to give. The following journal entry dated March 29, 2001, indicates that Inside child parts were relating to Jean rather than her adult partner: *I work hard inside to understand what Jean wants, and how to do that, and I think I've got it. But she says I am just pretending and my support is not real. So I guess I haven't got it again. I am very bad, that I can't get it right for her. But I don't know how. I worry about Jean, her sadness, her unhappiness that is mainly due to me. And, although I try very hard to do what she wants, I don't get it right. She says if I continue in the same way, in a year she can't promise we will be together because I have not been real, I've just been pretending. I don't know exactly what I have been doing wrong. But it certainly is wrong. Very wrong. And very bad. I am very bad. Very.*

Beginning therapy again also affected my work life. There were many triggers at work that took me back to the abuse. I felt that I had no control of the demands made of me at work, just as I had no control over the demands of my abusers. The unreasonable workload triggered the life-threatening desperation felt when I was tortured with impossible demands and horrifying consequences. I frantically tried to do all the work and meet all the demands. Picking up the phone and hearing a sudden verbal assault of an angry client triggered the terror of hearing my torturers' angry threats. I worked in a medical setting and occasionally had to tell a doctor that a treatment could not be done in a patient's home. This triggered the childhood terror of the inevitable torture that would result from saying "no" to an authority figure. Working with families where I suspected abuse triggered feelings of helplessness and an overwhelming sense that I was to blame for everything that went wrong.

Pat recommended that only the parts that knew the work would be present at work, and that all the other parts could have a safe place inside to stay, play, and do whatever they wanted to do. As the following journal entries from early May 2001 describe, I had difficulty having the right parts out at the right time: *It is hard to always have the right people out. Sometimes I can't seem to do that. I am not sure who the right one to have out is. Maybe that is what makes shopping so hard. I feel like no one is there, but maybe it is everyone. A few are trying to come out and they all get stuck in the door, so no one is really out. Sometimes the one who is present does not know where I am or the people I am with. Very often I have the feeling of disorientation and of being very scattered and unable to focus, like I am going in many directions yet going nowhere. ... I am getting to know my many different parts. There are so many. It can be overwhelming. I am trying to get the right one or ones out at the right time. The right ones sometimes get lost. Someone who might seem to be the right person is not right and doesn't respond or function as required. This is a horrible and embarrassing experience. I must appear to be insensitive, incompetent, and sometimes downright out to lunch.*

I occasionally considered applying for disability. I repeatedly decided not to apply because I feared that if I left work, I would never return. I took very few sick days for the same reason. As difficult as my job was, it did give me a different focus, and my colleagues were helpful and supportive. In retrospect, I think that having a routine, relationships with co-workers, responsibilities, and a sense of financial independence were important to my healing. The benefits outweighed the stresses of working.

Social interaction was difficult. In social gatherings, I felt awkward and out of place. I did not know what to say and I had difficulty focusing on conversations. I found it difficult to prepare a meal for company as I could not seem to remember what to do. As the following journal entry from May 2001 indicates, I was aware of my difficulty functioning in social situations, at work, and at home: *I can't seem to function very well anywhere. I take things literally. I see things like a child or children. I respond like a child who doesn't fit in an adult world. Jean says to let anyone out who wants to come out at home, but when I do, I hurt her or it's not what she wants. I can't seem to keep track of things. My mind is in a fog. Work is extremely hard. I must come across very oddly at times. When I get odd looks, I know I have said the wrong thing.*

I needed more and more time to listen to myself and to learn about the Inside. Even if I was with people, I closed down. I had an intense need to be alone a great deal of the time. It was difficult to meet this need because I worked and had a partner and a child. The parts, like small children, needed my time and attention and I had only limited time to give. Getting up early, writing, and running gave me some time alone. However, the need to be by myself and pay attention inside created conflicts within me and within my home.

After a few months of therapy, life seemed harder. I felt very tired. I had trouble filling my responsibilities. I worked very hard at everything, but I did not seem to accomplish what was needed. I felt like I was not making any progress. However, there were bright moments that would eventually become longer and more lasting: *Yesterday, when I was raking, it felt like I was seeing everything for the first time and how beautiful it was.*

I remained committed to the process of therapy. I was glad to find a therapist who had the skills to help me. Starting therapy again meant that I would slowly learn about the severity of the torture I had endured. The genius of dissociation is that I had no idea about the extent of the violence or what healing would require.

EIGHT

COMMUNICATION

I continued to identify families of parts on the Inside and to communicate with them. Pat continued to point out what a good job the parts had done and encouraged me to communicate this to the parts in order to develop a positive environment on the Inside. This positive self-regard encouraged further communication.

I was usually in a fair amount of distress before it was time to attend the next therapy session. There was a sense of losing my way and of not knowing what to do with many problems such as having a body memory, feeling intensely afraid or depressed, or having trouble functioning. I began most therapy sessions telling Pat about these problems. Pat would help me get in touch with the part or parts involved. "Ask Inside," she would invite. I learned to close off everything external and to focus on the internal. I knew that Pat was sitting across from me, but I did not look at her or even really see her office. My eyes were open, but I was not interacting with Pat. My attention was totally focused on listening to the Inside.

I was listening to my dissociated self. I could see the parts, and they felt very separate from me. Sometimes several talked at one time. Sometimes they were talking and I did not realize it. Sometimes I felt a pain in my body or an intense emotion. Sometimes I heard words. Sometimes I saw images.

Sometimes there did not seem to be any communication. Sometimes there was such a cacophony that I could not stand it.

When one part disclosed the trauma in which she had been created, another part immediately said that this was not true. This had also happened when I initially remembered in the mid-eighties. It was crazy. I did not know why I would hear about horrible things that happened to me and then hear that this could not be true. Most systems, said Pat, have parts that deny what happened. She emphasized that this was a vitally important job for survival.

I wrote about the importance of denial in July 2001: *The role of the denial family is to let me be in the world and relate to others. The violence is totally separate. … The deniers told me that there are many of them because the inside needs to be totally covered so nothing could get through to the outside. The deniers are in various positions including horizontal, vertical, and diagonal so that nothing can leak through. They have made it so I can exist in the world. They are very skilled. They do allow different people out in different situations, but with no thoughts, feelings, or memories of any bad things. Sometimes no feeling at all is the only way. They have allowed the creation of people with no memories of any abuse, to handle the present. When the outside was getting too close to the inside, the deniers directed distraction.*

I started to learn that my multitude of physical complaints was mostly communication from the parts. I felt a bone-weary exhaustion for most of my life. I frequently felt so worn out that I could not walk another step or do another thing. At the same time, I felt immense pressure to do much more. It never made sense. Why, as a child, a teenager, and in my twenties and early thirties, would I feel so exhausted? Perhaps keeping things so separate was exhausting. Perhaps, as Pat suggested, the exhaustion could be memories. It would be very exhausting for a child to be tortured at night and then go to school and pretend to herself and others that she was fine.

I wrote about chest pain. The Outside asked the Inside for help with the chest pain, which continued to be an issue for several years. On March 26, 2001, I wrote to the pain in my chest: *Hello everyone. You are doing great. Pain in my chest, what do you want? Pain in my chest, who are you? Cough. Big cough. Trouble breathing. Who are you? I love you. Pain in my chest you are making me hurt. Why? So I can't feel other things? Because I need love? When I breathe I hurt. Breathing isn't supposed to hurt.*

Breathe. Are you a part? Sudden headache. Eyes going funny. I know you are there. Where were you born? What is your job? You have all done a great job. So when the body could not breathe, I could go somewhere and keep breathing. How old are you? All ages. Weight on my chest. Breathe. Keep breathing. … Breathe. Weight, heavy on my chest. Pushed through to my back. Heaven. Death is OK. Gone. I am only the chest, no other body parts. Except for my arms, my head. Nothing below my chest. He hates me so much. I am so bad. BAD. BAD. BAD.

On April 1, 2001, someone wrote the following in capital letters: *CHEST—CAN'T BREATHE—GONE, WARM AIR BIRDS SUNNY. PUSHING ON CHEST TO BACK. DYING. GONE. BIG HAND ALL OVER. NO AIR. GONE. HAND OVER MOUTH. GONE. SKIN OUCH. BABY CRYING. CRY. CRY. CRY. CRY. GONE.*

Also on April 1, 2001, a very different someone wrote in my journal: *I feel like I have descended into a huge abyss. How do I recreate myself so that the abyss becomes a place of beauty and love so the sorrow and pain and loneliness and terror are transformed into strength and relationship and trust and love and energy and creativity? I am only starting to realize how many parts I have separated myself into. Can one remember at age, 4–6 months or younger? Is that possible? I don't know who it was at such an early age—just big hands—can't breathe.*

During therapy sessions, for most problems I presented, Pat would ask me to ask Inside for information. When the information was in the form of a traumatic memory, Pat would ask how old I was, where I was, my body position, what was happening to me, and what happened before and after the assault. I would focus on the Inside, and the information came in pieces. The pieces often came as physical sensations that did not initially make sense. Pat encouraged me to ask for help from other parts. It often took communication from several parts to understand that I was upside down or spinning or hanging or tied down. I was starting to recognize that many problems with my body did not make sense in the present. Rather, my body was giving me information about how I had been hurt.

I experienced intense emotion during the remembering, and I was grateful that it would be less intense when I asked to "turn down the volume." Sometimes I could tolerate only about 1 percent of the volume, or less. As the memory was fully recovered, the emotional pain would calm and the body pain would go away. If the pain did not go away, it meant there was more to remember.

I had always had a problem with constipation and with being able to urinate in a public washroom and sometimes at home. Journal entries from 2002 indicated that these problems were abuse related: *They never had a bowel movement for a very long time. They were shut down and scared to have a bm. They would not do it during abuse. They had to learn to not do it.* The constipation problem seemed to be because I had been forced to control my body in this way: *They wouldn't let me pee for a long time. … I learned not to pee or vomit or have a bowel movement if at all possible.* I started to understand that the abusers made me control my bodily functions in order to meet their sadistic requirements.

I had frequent headaches. They occurred when there was much anxiety or conflict. Sometimes I felt that Inside parts were holding on tightly to their roles, were in tense conflict with each other, and were not talking to me. I ignored the headaches as much as possible, because focusing on them did not help. As therapy progressed, the headaches subsided.

In September 2002 I wrote about knee pain with the realization that it was a memory: *I have very bad sudden pain in my knees. I feel like the Inside is saying that I can't walk. I was suddenly on my knees. I was blindfolded. Oh Daddy, my knees hurt. Where did my legs beneath my knees go? I can't feel them. I can't get up.*

I realized that the trouble I had staying awake while driving and while writing was due to parts putting me to sleep. It helped to understand that parts were doing a job they were trained to do. In order to stay awake while driving, I had to make sure that an older part who was the good driver was present. There was often a struggle Inside to stop the sleepy ones from coming out while driving. It took years to get all the memories relating to putting myself to sleep.

I could no longer function in the world as I used to. It was like parts interfered with my usual functioning. They would take over more. It was more difficult to stay focused on a particular task. I reacted as a child in adult situations. My problem with functioning "normally" was most acute at work. Pat suggested that I negotiate with the Inside so that only the adult parts of me who knew the job were out at work. All the other parts were encouraged to choose to go to a nice place Inside to protect them from worrying about what was happening at work. In May 2001 I wrote in an effort to ask parts to help me be able to function at work: *Lately, stress has resulted in difficulty functioning. I need everyone to help me do a good job. I need you to help me think as an adult, to relate to others as an adult, to remember to use my intelligence as an adult. I need all the children who have tried to be out at work to help me by letting the adult working ones be out at work. I will do my best to listen when I can. Let's work together to have a good day. I do love you all. I know I am not very good at showing it.*

Food and my weight had been constant obsessions for years. I had not considered that the Inside world might be contributing to this problem. I wrote about being anorexic in May 2002: *The anorexia is about a bunch of things. Thinking about food constantly means not thinking about other things and not having any feelings. Being anorexic gave me hope that, when I became thin enough, my life would be OK. Being consumed with thoughts related to food gave purpose, meaning. It was something I was good at. I could restrict myself like no one else I knew and people would comment about my self-control. I hated my body, and thought that not eating was well-deserved punishment. Anorexia was to do with control. I could control what I put in my mouth.* I learned that as a very young child, I was not fed for long periods of time. Sometimes, I was force-fed. As a teenager I was made to lose or gain weight, depending on the whims of the customers who paid my "parents" to assault me.

The problem of my mother surfaced occasionally in therapy. I felt better calling her SP2, an abbreviation for sadistic pedophile two. On the one hand, I did not want to have anything to do with her. On the other hand, I felt a pull toward her, a tendency to look after her and make sure her needs were met. I had been closer to her than to my father, SP1. I continued to feel intense fear when I received a card from her or when I heard about her from others. It slowly became clear to me that my mother did not care about me. She trained me to accept whatever was done to me and to never let out any clues about the abuse. I remembered that she encouraged my father, SP1, to abuse me. Sometimes she watched. SP2 trained me to deny that I was abused, particularly to myself. I did not understand until much later in therapy that SP2 was actually the one who directed SP1 to hurt me.

Pat's education about what constituted good parenting meant that I changed my view of SP2. I experienced intense sadness as I realized that my parents were not who I had thought they were. I was shocked when I started to understand that it was the job of the Outside to believe and act like I had good parents, in order to fool others and, most of all, myself. I wrote the following on March 10, 2002: *Such a cover-up. The one who was most fooled was me. The Outside had to believe a lie to survive. The separation from me hurts the most.*

I started to understand that the strong emotions I felt, those that did not seem to fit in the present, were emotional flashbacks. Inside parts were telling about what happened to them and what they did to help. I experienced overwhelming sadness, sometimes to the point of feeling so heartbroken I wondered if I could go on. September 13, 2002: *Parts weren't taking over totally, but were giving memories of feeling so alone and isolated and constantly feeling wrong, all wrong. There was utter desolation. A nothingness.*

The processing of past emotions meant changes that were positive on the one hand and very uncomfortable on the other. The Inside system, which was created to survive terror, was starting to comprehend that my current life had much less fear and terror. August 25, 2002: *I have moments of decreased anxiety. These moments can be quite anxiety-producing themselves, as the whole system is not used to any moments without anxiety and fear.*

My functioning at work was changing. Pat helped me to understand how a crisis-oriented job triggered the perpetrators' technique of forcing me to try to do the impossible, with the inevitable punishment for not doing as instructed. When I had some perspective, I understood that the problem was not the job but rather the ways that I had been abused. I did not have any rights when I was abused. It had not occurred to me that I had rights at work. Inside parts did not know that I had any rights. On July 21, 2002, I wrote: *I need to work out better ways of surviving at work. I feel uptight, like I cannot handle it. I am very insecure and lacking in confidence. Maybe this is a theme throughout my life. It is like I am suddenly being vaulted, via a time machine, into this life. I only vaguely know this life. I am not sure how to act, what to say, or what to do. I try to act normally, but I do not know what that is. I am not sure of anything.*

Pat taught me about the psychological effects of being tortured as a child. She emphasized that the pedophiles had intentionally created situations to cause the most extreme distress and terror. She explained how a child learns. She explained that a child believes what adults say. Pat pointed out repeatedly that I escaped, that I got away. In the following journal entry, dated June 10,

2002, I am writing to parts that are learning that the horror is over: *The Fear Family members, who are everywhere in the system, are always on guard. It is extremely difficult for them to hear—let alone understand—that we do not live in the horror anymore. They grew up from the very beginning in the horror. And they are instrumental to my sanity today. And they are to be loved, congratulated, and celebrated. They continue to live out of that horror mind-set. They anticipate horror at every turn, every day, all day. That is their normal.*

Improved communication brought the beginning of understanding. Pat's education about dissociation, about the process of remembering and of listening Inside, started to make sense. The idea that my parents had trained me to not consciously know about all the horror was hard to believe yet made perfect sense. I started to identify some of my perpetrators' techniques in training me to not consciously remember in order to protect themselves. While I often felt like I was in a life-and-death situation, Pat's frequent reaffirmation that I had escaped was starting to have an effect at deeper levels within my internal system. The hope that had always been there was growing.

NINE

YOU GOT AWAY

Contact with family members resulted in severe crises. Parts were on high alert. Instantly, I felt fear. I felt an uncomfortable sense that maybe my family does love me. At the same time, there was a frantic need to get away as well as well as deny the abuse. Conflicts collided and escalated. I had difficulty functioning. Current stresses were heard by terrified and frantic child parts who had no choices, no rights, and who had to do everything perfectly, knowing at the same time that they could not do anything right. This was followed by a blunt realization that there was no love and that by fear they were trying to get me back. I came to realize that I felt much better when I had no contact with any family members.

Telephone calls with my brother, Bruce, resulted in distress and inner conflicts. On the one hand, little parts Inside felt very protective of Bruce. They felt they had done all they could to protect him. They felt they loved him. They felt responsible for him. They felt tremendous heartbreak about leaving him. When he phoned they felt hopeful that maybe he does care. On the other hand, any contact with him was unsupportive, unhelpful, and triggering.

Bruce would phone repeatedly until he reached me. I answered so that I would not have to worry about him phoning for a while. As he talked about seemingly inane subjects like the weather and politics, the fear and conflict on the Inside escalated. Inside parts were terrified. As I described in my April 4,

2003, journal entry, they had been programmed to believe that the torturers could get to me through Bruce: *Whisper, pass it along. I am not supposed to speak out loud, but I can whisper. Whisper is not the same thing. I will get you no matter what. Through Mommy, Bruce, and family, I will reach out and get you. Even when no one is there, I will get you.* The psychological aftermath of these phone calls went on for days, as the guilt, terror, and denial collided.

I agreed to meet Bruce in October 2002; he was in a nearby city on business. My anticipatory anxiety was very high. I did not want to see him. I had a panic attack driving to meet him. In spite of my state of anxiety, I asked Bruce what he remembered about the abuse. This resulted in an immediate and severe crisis: *Deniers are much stronger after seeing Bruce. I must have made it all up. It was just an ordinary family. I did have comfort and enjoyment watching TV with Bruce.*

The day after seeing Bruce, I wrote: *Feel like I can hardly go on. Takes more effort than what I have. No one seems to notice. Total overload at work and I don't know how to handle it. Chaos Inside. Deniers are very strong. They want to go back, to where there was no knowledge of the system and no connection. I had a family then. I had parents and brothers. I had no knowledge that anything was wrong. Yet I had depression, anorexia, and a desperate need to make it better. But there was a semblance of family, like everyone else. When I asked Bruce for acknowledgment of the abuse, all systems crashed. Run for cover. Heartbreak, loss, sadness. Pushing over the edge. More and more difficult to function. Totally done in. Not safe anywhere. I am the closest to safe with Jean.*

In response to this crisis, Pat suggested that I change my internal system, which I wrote about as follows: *The inside system is recreating itself based on the truth rather than on the lies that I was told. The system is built on cooperation, not separateness. It is based on knowing each other and helping each other. It is based on communicating feelings, thoughts, opinions, and ideas. It is a place where kids grow up safe, happy, and have what they need.*

I had great distress when I received Bruce's written response to my question. On November 10, 2002, I wrote about my response to his letter: *Letter from Bruce on Friday. He says he can't acknowledge that I was abused. He says he has no memory of any abuse. He says that he can see that something has affected me greatly. Why does he not believe me when I say what the problem is?*

I wrote to Bruce telling him to call me when he remembered about the abuse. The adults in the system had decided that no contact was best as long as Bruce continued to deny any abuse. With no contact from Bruce, the little parts that were protective of Bruce would eventually be able to tell about witnessing Bruce being abused. I was able to undo programming I had received that the assaults Bruce experienced were my fault. This was heartbreaking work.

Indirect contact with my mother caused intense internal distress. Hearing from a distant relative who kept in contact with my mother was very distressing. I felt that my mother could get to me through relatives. I felt instant panic when I saw the name of a brother or cousin on the telephone display. When I listened to a message from a relative saying he or she would phone back, the anxiety and panic lasted for days.

Receiving a Christmas or birthday card with my mother's writing on the envelope caused intense panic. My partner agreed to open all such cards and letters. She found them innocuous, but she respected my need not to read them. In time, I came to understand that everyday words like "mother," "love," and "family" were trigger words intended to reactivate the "never-leave" programming.

It took many years in therapy to let myself see that my "parents" were not people who put my needs first and helped to prepare me for the best possible life. In therapy I learned about how good parents treat their children and about the need for children to proceed through developmental stages. I began to understand that my parents never intended to do their best to provide what I needed to grow physically and to develop emotionally, cognitively, and spiritually. It took several more years to understand that my parents intended to train me to be a willing participant in assaults by sadistic pedophiles.

My lack of knowledge and skills to be independent in the world puzzled me. Why had my parents not taught me about cooking, cleaning, laundry, ironing, finances, going to school, getting a job, and finding out about my talents and interests? There were many things in my relationships with my parents that did not make sense. Why did I cringe when my mother came near me? Why did I not want to see her? Why did she not care that I was suicidal? Why was I so relieved when my father died?

On the one hand, my reaction to contact with family members did not make any sense. On the other hand, the reactions were so strong that I could not have any contact. The system Inside was making sure that I got away. While I was not yet ready to know all the reasons why my family was so terrifying, I could not ignore the fear and I had to get away from them.

I initially "got away" after my father's death in 1982. I continued to "get away" from that time on. Learning the truth about what happened to me helped me to get more completely away. I realized that my mother and father were parents in name and appearance only. Parenting was their cover, to give them legitimate possession of me.

Pat repeated to me countless times, "You got away." This reminded all the parts that I was no longer in the abusive situation. It reminded all of me that I had gone against the programming to never leave and the programming to die if I left. The healing wisdom of the Inside had pushed me out of the family situation. I had gotten away from the sadistic pedophiles in the sense that I no longer saw them. I had not yet gotten away from them in the sense that they had programmed my mind to do their bidding.

TEN

DEPROGRAMMING

I had layers of intricate programming that the trainers, including SP1 and SP2, started when I was an infant and continued until I got away. Their goal was to have total control of my mind. The purpose of the programming was to force me to create dissociated parts that did as instructed by the trainers. This programming was totally dissociated from my consciousness. The quiet, smiling, pleasing child who lived in such a seemingly normal suburban home and went to school each morning knew nothing about being prostituted to vicious men, being victimized during ritualistic sadistic orgies, or being made the subject of violent pornographic pictures and films.

There was programming not to tell, not to leave, to commit suicide, and to willingly participate in extreme sadistic/masochist sexual acts. I was programmed to believe that the trainers were always watching me and knew everything that I thought, did, and said. Customers paid for the specialized acts that I was programmed to perform. They paid for pictures and movies of me being sexually assaulted. There was backup after backup programming so that if one program failed, another would get the job done. Programming was triggered by words, looks, phone calls, situations, noises, and direct commands.

Programming always started with trauma. I was deprived of food, drink, sleep, warmth, light, people, and the freedom to move. Drugs altered my state of consciousness and paralyzed me. I was tortured with electrical shocks and by sadistic sexual and physical assaults. There were elaborate situations where I witnessed what I perceived to be murders and decapitations. I was forced to drink what I was told was blood and to eat what I was told was human flesh.

When I was cold, hungry, drugged, overwhelmed with physical agony, hopeless, and wanting to die, I was receptive for the programming. I was taught to never tell. I was programmed to never leave. I was programmed to suicide if I could not stop myself from leaving. I was taught how to talk to a customer. I was programmed to act like I wanted to be the victim of sadistic pedophiles. I was programmed to believe that I was responsible for the tortured state of others. I was forced to hurt animals and humans because I was told if I did not do it, they would be hurt even worse.

I came to realize that my body memories, emotional memories, and obsessions or compulsions were telling me about programming. In therapy sessions, I would present a body pain, emotional distress, or an obsessive thought, and Pat instructed me to ask Inside for more information. I usually denied that my problem had anything to do with programming and talked about my distress. Pat kept me focused by asking where I was, how old I was, what body position I was in, what was done to me, what I was told, and what happened before and after the programming. She often repeated, "We have to get the programming,," or the problem would continue.

I was intensely afraid of learning about the trauma that was always involved in the programming. Pat would remind me to "turn down the volume" of the intensity. I usually chose 1 percent of the volume. As I said out loud what had happened to me, Pat encouraged me to say as much as I could by asking, "What happened next?" and "Is there anything more?" These questions felt gentle and caring. I did not feel forced to remember or tell. After parts had told about what the trainers did to me and the message that was put into my head, Pat suggested that I thank them and care for them, and that they could choose another job when they were ready to do so.

I knew that Pat could handle hearing about the terrifying, horrible assaults. She seemed familiar with the depravity of the assaults. She normalized the types of torture and my horror. She also knew that my perspective was often that of a very young child who would believe anything, and that adults can trick children into believing whatever they choose.

The foundational programming as an infant and a toddler was the most difficult to undo. I needed to understand why programming an infant is so effective. Pat explained about infants and toddlers being totally dependent on their adult caregivers. A very young child has to do what the adult makes them do. There is no choice. A very young child is totally vulnerable to the adult and is also learning a great deal. An adult who is trained in programming can make the child's mind split at a very early age. Infant and toddler parts do not communicate by words. I created birds inside my system that helped communication with the infants. The birds could translate the messages from and to the infants. This helped a lot. I was, however, impatient with the necessary slowness of the communication.

My right heel hurt for years. This was due to programming started as an infant. On October 14, 2002, I made my first journal entry about heel pain: *Parts have been telling me for some time about the very sore right heel on the bottom of my foot. It is like a thumb pressing hard right on bone, it is very sore.* I thought that my foot orthotic must be the problem and had it adjusted, but the heel pain intensified. Pat helped me to realize that this pain was from body memories.

In November 2002 I wrote about learning that SP1 and SP2 tortured me so I would be silent and still: *Body memories. Sore heel. Prick. Electric shock. Core split. Very young. Split from core. Anger family was the first family. When the heel of right foot pricked there was a flash and intense pain everywhere. This was likely electrical current to teach me not to cry, not to react, and not to fight back. They shocked me when I cried and stopped when I was quiet. If I was crying, they just had to touch my heel and I stopped. I refuse to let fear colour all that I do, all that I am. Let go of the fear. Express the anger in a contained way. I am becoming a whole me.* Pat said she thought they created me for all the torture rather than to grow up to have a good life. I came to understand that I did not have to keep the heel programming: *They taught us that they would forever hurt and terrorize us. But they lied. They hurt us in so many ways. We wanted to believe they would do something good, but they always seemed to hurt us. Heel programming was to stop crying and not to move. Do not need to keep the heel pain. Can let it go. Give it back to those horrible criminals.*

Pat suggested looking after the little parts. I focused on a three-year-old part. In January 2003 I wrote about the multicoloured wheelchair I created in my imagination for a three-year-old part whose foot was hurt: *The little girl still needs to be reminded to use the multicoloured electric wheelchair. She has adult parts helping her, playing with her, looking after her, gently loving her. She likes the wheelchair and loving the attention. I sleep much better now. Things seem clearer.* The little girl in the wheelchair held emotional pain: *Feelings of intense sorrow from the 3 year old. Heartbreaking sorrow. Intense rage. He said that he would always have a link to my heel to give me pain.*

The little part with the hurt foot knew I was hoping to write a book, and I realized how important it was to know what had happened to me: *She is ready to give the multicoloured wheelchair away. The 3 year old little girl wants to be in my book. The little girl has lots of tears. They pressed on the nail and twisted it when she did not do what they wanted. I was so afraid of the memories. I didn't want to know, but working through the memories is the way to freedom.* The little part was healing: *The little girl is doing much better. She can play and does happy things. She eats because she feels hungry and she enjoys it. She is learning to trust the adult inside. She is able to get extremely angry at SP1 and SP2.*

My partner, Jean, remembered that when SP2 had visited, she talked about her shoes and feet. I remembered thinking at the time that this subject did not really fit into the conversation. I realized that it is likely she was trying to activate the heel programming.

There were programs to keep on creating more parts who would keep the heel pain going. In therapy, I processed the memories and looked after the tortured parts just as I had looked after the part with the multicoloured wheelchair. For several years, the heel pain would appear. I would listen and process more of the programming until I no longer had heel pain.

I had body memories of excruciating teeth pain. For several mornings I had pain in my teeth that would last about ten minutes. On November 27, 2005, I wrote: *Lately, for the last few weeks, I have been having pain in my teeth. It has to do with programming from an infant and older as well. Very painful insertions on the gums make the whole jaw excruciatingly painful. This programming was about not crying. It was about silencing that initial fight-back response that all creatures are born with.*

During one therapy session I described feeling very disoriented. Pat asked if I was spinning. Yes, that was it. I was spinning. On February 23, 2003, I wrote: *He wanted my mind to be constantly spinning in terror about things that I could do nothing about. My mind kept the fear spinning, telling myself that I did that wrong, I had to do it right, but I did not know what right was. There was no way to get it right, but I had to get it right. The desperate push to do the impossible kept spinning, which kept the anxiety and terror alive at all times.*

I remembered physically spinning on a variety of pieces of equipment including a spit that rotated. I described what that felt like in an April 2, 2003, journal entry: *I had been thinking that I was heading toward a stroke. I had headaches and felt that my head would explode. I felt pressure all over my body but nothing was touching me. The room was spinning on a couple of occasions recently. I was spun to silence me and to thoroughly train me. As I talked about the spinning in therapy, my vision markedly improved. I was relieved that I was not going to have a stroke. Sometimes my speech is poor, too.*

With each memory of spin programming, Pat asked me what the position of my body was, how old I was, and what was happening to me, including what was being said to me. The purpose of the spinning on the Outside was to spin on the Inside and send the programming throughout the system. Deprogramming the spin programs meant that all that was spun throughout the system was undone. The programs were to keep quiet, to not get away, and to hate myself at every level.

After several years of therapy, my voice changed. People often commented that I had a sore throat. I could not say what I needed and wanted to say. There was much more to say. It seemed like my voice was trying hard to silence me. On November 27, 2005, I wrote about the purpose of voice programming: *To get rid of my voice, that crying voice, the voice that made any sound. Mouth kept open, jaw very sore, no voice at all, to get rid of that initial reaction against assault so that, out of terror, they take complete control over my instinctive reactions.*

I learned that there were many traumas to my throat including swallowing things that choked and burned. I was strangled until I passed out. I remembered being forced to witness a man's throat being cut, because he supposedly told what he was not supposed to tell. I was programmed to believe that the sadistic pedophiles knew every word I said. I continued to process all the voice programming.

Pat helped me to process the torture sessions in which I was programmed to never leave. If this programming failed and I left, I was programmed to always go back or commit suicide. I realized that the cards, phone calls, and family visits were all about activating the "never-leave" programming. This programming included much about what happened to others who left. The message was that those who escaped returned and were endlessly tortured. If they did not return, they were programmed to commit suicide. I wrote on March 15, 2003: *When somebody says the words "your mother" to me, I feel instant fear. I hear the words "I will always find you. I will always get you back." What does that mean? Someone is afraid that they'll find us, drag us back to the violence and terror.*

After much deprogramming, I was healing, I was becoming more myself. Unfortunately, this led to further suicide programming. In April 2006 I realized: *It is like each step of becoming more me brings an equal and opposite reaction of resistance from the programming to prevent me from being me. To even exist now, at age 52 and two months, is a big no-no. I was never supposed to live this long. Once I was deemed totally useless and lost, suicide or being murdered was my only fate. Suicide would be preferable, as my murder would be used to torture others I cared about. So now the goal is get all the suicide programming. I do not feel suicidal. I want to live. I want to learn. I do not want to kill myself. Suicide programming changes that almost instantly. There are many cues to kill myself. Hearing that someone else killed themselves is a cue. Words like family, mother, and love lead to the programming that I am the worst possible person, that I have done the worst things any human being can do and I must kill myself before anyone else is harmed because of me.*

Pat kept asking about more suicide programming. Sometimes I thought that there was not any left. Eventually, faint thoughts of suicide would become stronger and difficult to resist. Thankfully, the parts that stopped me from killing myself were also getting stronger. They developed a way of contracting with the suicidal parts to not suicide now, and to reconsider in a few months. This gave me time to get help. Sometimes this meant a crisis call to Pat. Sometimes I wrote. Sometimes I promised myself I would talk about it in my next therapy session. Once it was identified and processed, the suicidal thoughts went away.

As deprogramming continued, I realized that I had a great deal to live for. I was not ready to die. I hoped I had many decades left in my life. My resolve strengthened to free myself from the mind control used by the criminals who stole so much from me. Growing stronger had two results. First, I learned to recognize when suicide programming had been activated and to turn it off by myself or with Pat's help. Second, I was getting to the worst of the programming.

ELEVEN

THE WORST OF IT

I was starting to consciously understand what had been intentionally done to me. I felt more confident in my abilities to help myself learn about the horrors I had endured. It was important to listen to the parts' experiences. Parts needed to communicate the terror of what they had experienced and to be believed. Then they needed to be cared for and kept safe in places that I created in my imagination.

I learned how to "turn down the volume" when I worked through a memory. I asked Inside to reduce the intensity of the emotional pain. I explained that I would not be able to continue with the memory if the emotions were too intense. Parts knew that they had taken the original horror because I could not handle it. The parts understood that reducing the intensity allowed me to learn what happened and release the emotion. Even if the emotion was reduced to 1 percent, it was still effective in releasing it. "Turning down the volume" was crucial as I worked through deeper and more horrifying layers of memories.

As a toddler, a part was programmed to never leave by seeing the head of a child explode and hearing agonizing screams because she tried to leave. The part believed that this child's head had been shot and severed because the child tried to leave. This part of me needed to tell about this experience and how terrifying it was. Pat instructed older parts to see what was happening. Older parts were necessary because the younger part did not have the ability to understand that this scenario was a trick. The realizations came that I was seeing it all from a drugged perspective, that it was pumpkin pulp and seeds, not a human brain that splattered, and that the screams were on a tape recorder. Because I was so young and in an altered state I believed what I experienced, even if it was a trick.

The programming always included self-blaming for the suffering of others. It was always the little part's fault. So along with the horror of witnessing a child's head exploding, the part was convinced that it was her fault that the child tried to leave and had to suffer. This part needed to learn that the torturers had made the "head" explode and blamed her to make sure the programming was even more effective.

Pat had suggested the creation of therapy teams in order to help all the parts to be free of the horror and to grow up and choose another job. I reminded myself about this as I wrote in my journal on October 13, 2004: *Therapy teams will give lots of attention and care for parts as they tell what happened to them. Parts can express their feelings knowing they are safe and cared for. After parts tell of the horror they can start to heal and learn to enjoy life. They will learn that life now is good, safe and that those horrors do not happen now.*

I came to understand the importance of the "Heroines," a family of parts who were trained to perform acts that were requested by customers who paid for extremely sadistic acts. It was important for the system to acknowledge how important the "Heroines" were to survival and how hurt they were. On June 9, 2004, I wrote about these parts: *The Heroines are very important to everyone. They are very crucial, critical parts. Heroines were convinced that they like the sexual feelings, the turn-on, the humiliation, the pain. The Heroines liked cleaning up his urine, desperately begged him to pee on the floor because they really needed a drink. When they licked it up he would rape me from behind. You are wonderful. You did what had to be done. You are beautiful, strong, intelligent, creative, and extremely courageous.*

The "Heroines," who were the torturers' reason for all the training, also bore much of the heartbreaking shame of the whole system. On October 14, 2004, I wrote about understanding the truth about the "Heroines": *These raunchy, sexually aggressive parts were made to do horrible things and look like they enjoyed it.*

Their shame is overwhelming. Did they really "enjoy" the pain? They thought they did. They had to play the part to try to prevent worse. Worse usually happened anyway.

The "Heroines" had so much shame and heartbreak. They needed to tell how they were forced to behave as they did so they could heal and grow up. They needed much tender loving care, safety, and love. A beautiful place was created for them. And their importance was explained to the rest of the system.

Suicide programs were activated by the healing. Pat frequently asked about suicide programming and helped to process the programming memory. The healing teams also helped with this and could be on the lookout for more suicide programming. On October 12, 2004, I encouraged the parts to help undo this programming: *Yes, there are suicide programs. That is what landmines are. The feelings of peacefulness, contentment, and confidence are triggers to suicide programs. So parts have been trying to protect us. Again, a great job. How did they put that in there? What is the programming? Equate not feeling terror, anxiety, or dread with dying. I must find a way to die. Equate any sense of wholeness with dying. There is an overwhelming urge to die. Therapy teams look after parts and help to create healing programs. Spin love, attention, calmness. Give choice. Create a safe place. Broadcast that they have grown up and are living in safe place now. Lots of praise, attention.*

One of the most painful realizations was that my parents were not who I had always thought they were. I grieved the loss of parents I never had. I learned how I had created an image of my parents that I needed in order to survive, one that served me well until after I escaped. I slowly came to terms with the fact that my parents were sadistic trainers. I wrote about this change in perspective on August 28, 2005: *I so wanted them to be loving, good parents. I willed them to be good parents to fool, most of all, myself. I desperately needed to see them as caring parents, not as perpetrators of ritual abuse. Now, I am saying good-bye to the beliefs about my parents so that all of me can grow up and be me. I can see the truth of my past and present.*

I came to understand that SP1's and SP2's purpose was to stop me caring for others in order to save myself. On June 2, 2005, I wrote about my realization that my parents wanted me to become a sadistic pedophile or die: *All the trauma and programming was about fearing them. It was about being terrified for every second of life. It was about fearing everyone else because anyone could be one of them. I have moments when I feel really myself. I feel very comfortable, good, and strong. I am settled into myself, not scattered.*

The most difficult layer of the memory work was learning what I had done to others. This was my breaking point. I had tortured children, adults, and animals. I felt that I could not live with myself knowing what I had done to others. This was intended to destroy my soul. My capacity to create parts allowed my soul to be protected rather than destroyed. Thankfully, I was able to maintain that iota of myself that was horrified at the pain of others even at the expense of such heartbreak.

Jean and Pat helped me at this agonizing time. I remember Jean telling me, through my inconsolable tears, that she loved me no matter what, including what I had been forced to do to others. It was clear to me how much she loved me, and this helped me to live with myself. Pat was very clear that when one is coerced into hurting another, it is the fault of the coercer.

I had many pregnancies. I remembered many miscarriages and one almost full-term birth. I was not allowed to carry any pregnancy past three months, with one exception. When I was fourteen, I was pregnant to almost full term. On April 14, 2004, I wrote about the pregnancy: *Body was big, much bigger than now. I was both ashamed of my size and not in my body. At the same time, I did not realize that my body was swelling. I certainly did not know why. Intense pain. I thought he was inflicting it from somewhere else. I tried to tune it out. The baby was like a monkey, red-slimy, black hair, squirming. Even when I saw the baby, it did not feel real. She took it. Cry. Gurgle. Nothing. Gone. Now my belly swells with memories of the baby. Lower back pain—right in middle—related to pregnancy."*

The memory of this baby's birth returned over several years. I realized that I had killed my baby. This was more than I could tolerate. Pat helped me to remember all that had happened. I learned that the gurgle and sound of air I heard was the baby being killed by the sadistic pedophile. I was forced to stab the dead baby and forced to believe that I had killed it. Pat again explained that if a person is coerced into hurting another, it is the coercer who is responsible. This explanation meant I could eventually put the blame on the torturers and not myself. On February 7, 2007, I wrote about what I had deeply buried in my mind: *Yesterday, with Pat, I heard myself say that I cut my baby's throat at age 14 so that he wouldn't get tortured by a hot poker in the mouth and up the bum. Tremendous repulsion at myself. Both Pat and Jean say that the pedophiles were to blame. They made me do it and were responsible.*

There were so many memories that it seemed like therapy could be endless. Pat suggested stacking the memories by grouping the same type of assaults together and processing them together. Therapy teams could process one memory of the same kind of assault and then let me know the main points of each type of assault. Stacking the memories increased the pace of the processing.

My fear was subsiding. Parts that had told what had happened to them were free to do a healing job. There were new jobs like being positive, seeing beauty, laughing, being self-confident, and enjoying life. It was somewhat difficult to get used to these new experiences. It was very different to not be full of fear and feel like my life was at stake all the time. It was odd to feel peaceful inside. It was unusual to trust all the remaining parts, to trust myself, and to feel love for myself.

I remember my last therapy session. I did not have anything left to say. I felt peaceful and content. Pat asked, "Are we finished?" And I replied, "Yes." The day I had thought would never come had snuck up on me.

TWELVE

JEAN

J ean and I met in 1986. She was friendly, outgoing, and very kind. The
wisdom from the Inside could tell that Jean was not afraid of multiplicity.
The little parts trusted her. I felt comfortable with her. I needed a trustworthy
person who loved me. Jean accepted me. Most of me loved her and wanted to
make a life with her.

Jean likes children. She raised her three children and has grandchildren
and great-grandchildren. My Inside parts knew that she liked children and felt
safe with her. Jean believes that it is important to love children in order to live
with someone who is multiple. Jean recognized when my child parts came out.
She thought the parts were sweet and funny and that they needed her love.
She was right. It surprised us both how much all of me trusted her. It was also
a surprise to both of us when I agreed to move with Jean to be closer to her
family.

Jean told me that that my child parts behaved differently in a social setting than with just the two of us. They would take over. Although I looked
like an adult, I was behaving like a child. The child parts' fear of people and
their immaturity would occasionally come out with friends and Jean's family.
A child does not understand the complexity of adult communication. I said
inappropriate things and could not understand the reactions of others. Jean
covered for me when this happened. She would make a joke or redirect the

conversation. Fortunately, I was usually quiet, so Jean did not have to smooth things over too often.

Jean has commented that, sometimes, living with me was like looking after a troubled child. At other times, Jean felt I was one hundred years old and that I looked after her. Jean has said that I tried to look after her even when she did not need help. I was often very afraid of losing Jean, and my assessment of what Jean needed was magnified by that fear. I was also very protective of Jean.

Jean struggled to help me when I encountered an abusive boss and the stress increased to paranoia. I had to be with Jean all the time. I could not be by myself. This was difficult as Jean had a job. Jean called me her shadow, and she was afraid to leave me alone. Jean tried to sort out ways that I would not be alone. She said that it was very difficult knowing that I was constantly scared to death and that she could not be with me every minute. After I was out of the stressful situation for a few weeks, the paranoia resolved and Jean no longer had me as a shadow.

We raised Jean's granddaughter, Laurie, for a few years. The first four years were quite pleasant. Laurie's problems as a teenager coincided with my escalating problems. I reacted to Laurie's frustration and anger as a frightened child, particularly when she directed her anger at Jean. For the first time since Jean and I lived together, I felt unsafe in our home. This caused a severe crisis within me. Jean found that she was responsible for a troubled teenager and a troubled partner.

The worst problem for Jean during this crisis occurred when I did not know her and was afraid of her. Jean did not know what to do. Jean later understood that a part who did not know her had taken over. Jean decided that all she could do was go along with this part because she believed that it would change. Jean learned not to get too involved because eventually parts would change and the fear would go away. Jean also learned that it was better that I did not know she was upset, as this exacerbated my distress.

Jean later told me that when I became afraid of her, we lost the sense of "you and I together can fix anything" that we always had. This deeply bothered her. She felt lost. She decided that all she could do was know that whatever happened would happen and things would turn out the way they were supposed to, because she did not know what else to do.

Jean struggled with my intense anxiety and depression. "It drove me nuts," Jean admitted. "It was generally over nothing in the present. I tried to totally ignore the depressed parts." My depressed parts were only nominally present when we first got together. Jean does not like living with a depressed person. When I was depressed, my actions, statements, and feelings did not make sense to Jean, who did not see anything to be depressed about.

Jean is someone who needs to be needed. This need helped her to understand and accept my problems. When I did not need her, Jean felt lost and alone. Jean did not feel she should talk to anyone else about my problems because she was protecting me. Since Jean needed support, this decision made the situation even more painful for her.

When I started therapy again, Jean felt very left out. Jean felt that she had lost me. Jean needed some help, too, and did not know where to get it. It was a lonely time for Jean. She decided to wait it out. Slowly, Jean started to see some changes. It was a very long process. I would come home from a therapy session and say that maybe I was getting near the end of needing therapy. After the next therapy session I would tell her that there was a lot more. Jean felt angry at the length of time therapy took and at never knowing when things would be better.

Jean was very angry with my parents. She sometimes also found it very hard not to be angry with me. Jean was not getting what she needed and wanted out of the relationship. Jean reminded herself that I had limitations because of the severe trauma I had experienced. Jean thinks that most people are abused in some way and that we all have our limitations. Jean reflects that her limitations had been a problem in a previous relationship. Her conclusion is that "we all settle to some extent."

Jean felt that I would get better. She assumed that because I had made it this far, I would make it the rest of the way. While there were some days when Jean wondered if she would make it, she always thought that I would make it through. It took a lot longer than she would have liked. So many times, Jean made suggestions that she knew would help, but I did not accept the suggestion until someone else said it. Jean learned not to get upset about that.

As therapy progressed, Jean saw me changing. My sense of humour was more evident. The child parts were not out very much. Jean missed them. I seemed happier. I was more able to cope and switched less often. I was more adult, and there were fewer childlike reactions and much less "going nuts." All of the problems gradually got better.

I told Jean only a small amount of the details that I was remembering. This was enough to really scare her. She wondered if I was in danger. Jean wondered if she was in danger. Would writing a book endanger me more? These were horrible people. What are they capable of now? Jean worried for my safety. Jean's worry calmed when she saw that I did not seem that worried and nothing threatening happened.

I asked Jean what would have helped her when I was going through seven years of therapy for ritual abuse. Her summary follows:

1. Accept things the way they are. Know that things will not be right for a long time, so do not expect them to be.

2. Know that change is the one thing you can be sure of. Your partner will always change. Some changes will not make sense. Others might not see the changes, but if you live with a multiple person, you will see the changes. The changes may be quicker if the person is stressed. Try to understand and go with the flow. Stand back and roll with the changes. Try not to take the changes too seriously. You have to learn to live with the changes in order to stay in the relationship.

3. Make sure your partner knows you care. All of her needs to know this. As a child she was not loved and cared for. Your love and kindness will help in her healing.

4. Do not expect much of your partner while she is in the early stages of therapy.

5. Try to keep life as normal as possible. Socialize. Keep up with some activities, even though it is hard. Try to do something special. Try to make things seem normal with friends.

6. Have good support for yourself.

7. Have hope that your partner will improve and that the relationship will improve.

THIRTEEN

HEALING

Healing means ongoing learning. I learned that the hurt parts inside needed to experience safety and love. The parts needed to tell me what had happened to me and to express their pain to me. I needed to learn how to live with this new knowledge about myself.

Healing means learning to love all of me, including all of the Outside and the Inside. With the self-love that has grown over the years, most parts have grown up and merged into the whole. They can easily separate again if needed. Sometimes I need parts to help with unfinished healing of the trauma. Sometimes I need to remember what I have overcome. Communication among all of me is immediate. There is no separation between the Outside and the Inside. Under severe stress, parts sometimes become younger and temporarily separate to receive needed attention. To love myself means accepting all of me and my ongoing healing.

I also learned to accept the love of others. Jean was vital to my healing. She loved me. Her love is the most important of the many gifts I have been given. I felt safe with her. Our home was a refuge of safety. She was always there for me. Her presence in my life gave a context to the healing. Her acceptance of all my parts was important to their healing. In addition, members of Jean's extended family, our friends, and my co-workers have given me much-needed love and kindness. Most of these people did not know I was working through being ritually abused. Intuitively, with caring and kindness, there were many who gave me hope and love that helped me to continue to listen to the Inside. And at just the right times, our beloved dog and cats also offered their love.

I needed to work with a good, knowledgeable, and experienced therapist. Telling the truth to Pat, my trusted therapist, made healing possible. Pat believed me from the start. She helped me hear the truth from myself. She knew how to talk to the Inside parts to give them the information they needed about healing. Pat was willing to bear witness to the horror and heartbreak. She was available for telephone calls when horrible memories were coming and I could not cope. Over seven years of sessions every two weeks, Pat listened to me and helped me to find myself. She taught me to be my own therapist so that I am able to process any further memories.

I needed to accept the truth that the parts held. I accepted how harmful some human beings are. Such human beings appear to be normal. They know that most people do not want to consider that anyone would intentionally torture vulnerable children. Sadistic pedophiles take pleasure in trampling on the rights and needs of others. They enjoy the pain of their victims. They use the majority's disbelief about the worst of humanity to hide and continue their crimes. Neighbours would not comprehend that my parents, an ordinary looking professional couple, were members of an organized criminal group that trained me to be victimized by people who paid to torture me and to film and photograph their crimes. The more that people accept that there are people like my parents among us, the harder it is for them to commit their crimes.

I think that healing is an ongoing creative spiritual process. The process begins before this life and continues from this life to after. The process in this life includes learning about the divine within. I have always known that I had help from beyond this world. As healing continues, I am often made aware of the spirit that connects me to myself, others, and places beyond this world.

Healing is about giving back. I hope that this book helps therapists in their work with clients who have been terrorized as children. I hope that this book gives survivors encouragement to continue their healing. I believe that such healing brightens the much-needed hope for the safety, protection, and love of all who are in need.